Cambridge

Elements in Psyc~~
edi~
Kennet~ ~.
University of San Diego

INTERCULTURAL LEARNING THROUGH STUDY ABROAD

Susan B. Goldstein
University of Redlands

CAMBRIDGE
UNIVERSITY PRESS

CAMBRIDGE
UNIVERSITY PRESS

University Printing House, Cambridge CB2 8BS, United Kingdom

One Liberty Plaza, 20th Floor, New York, NY 10006, USA

477 Williamstown Road, Port Melbourne, VIC 3207, Australia

314–321, 3rd Floor, Plot 3, Splendor Forum, Jasola District Centre,
New Delhi – 110025, India

103 Penang Road, #05–06/07, Visioncrest Commercial, Singapore 238467

Cambridge University Press is part of the University of Cambridge.

It furthers the University's mission by disseminating knowledge in the pursuit of
education, learning, and research at the highest international levels of excellence.

www.cambridge.org
Information on this title: www.cambridge.org/9781009126960
DOI: 10.1017/9781009127011

First published 2022

A catalogue record for this publication is available from the British Library.

ISBN 978-1-009-12696-0 Paperback
ISSN 2515-3986 (online)
ISSN 2515-3943 (print)

Intercultural Learning through Study Abroad

Elements in Psychology and Culture

DOI: 10.1017/9781009127011
First published online: April 2022

Susan B. Goldstein
University of Redlands

Author for correspondence: Susan B. Goldstein, Susan_Goldstein@redlands.edu

Abstract: Over the past three decades, the population of international students throughout the world has steadily increased. Although university students choose to study in locations other than their home country for a variety of reasons, including professional development and disciplinary training, nearly all education abroad programs have intercultural learning as a central goal. In this Element, perspectives derived from cross-cultural psychological research are applied to an investigation of the effectiveness of study abroad as a mechanism for intercultural learning. Effectiveness is broadly defined and includes not only overall favorable program outcomes, such as gains in intercultural skills, knowledge, attitudes, and awareness, but also a recognition that study abroad experiences and outcomes may vary depending upon participants' diverse and intersectional identities. Best practices for facilitating intercultural learning through study abroad are identified, and strategies are outlined for addressing the methodological challenges of research in this area.

Keywords: study abroad, student mobility, intercultural competence, intercultural learning, international education

ISBNs: 9781009126960 (PB), 9781009127011 (OC)
ISSNs: 2515-3986 (online), 2515-3943 (print)

Contents

1 Introduction and Key Concepts

Over the past three decades, universities, professional associations, and national governments have recognized the need to prepare students for life and work in an increasingly diverse and global context, with rationales spanning economic, political, sociocultural, and educational concerns (de Wit & Altbach, 2021). Skrefsrud (2021, p. 63) explained, "As the speed and scale of migration and globalization changes societies, students need to develop the capacity to analyse and comprehend global issues, and learn how to interact respectfully with one another despite their cultural differences." Consistent with this perspective, the development of intercultural competence has become a central learning objective for postsecondary students across the globe (de Wit & Altbach, 2021; Griffith et al., 2016).

Conceptualizations of intercultural competence (ICC) vary considerably as they stem from multiple academic disciplines and may include as many as 325 different facets (Spitzberg & Changnon, 2009). Yet there is considerable agreement among scholars that ICC tends to be, at least to some extent, culture-general in nature (Arasaratnam & Doerfel, 2005) and includes cognitive (e.g., intercultural knowledge and awareness of cultural differences), affective (e.g., motivation for intercultural contact and nonjudgmental respect for unfamiliar cultures), and behavioral (e.g., the ability to obtain and appropriately apply cultural information; Behrnd & Porzelt, 2012; Deardorff, 2006; Root & Ngampornchai, 2013) components. Thus, Bennett (2008, p. 97) defined intercultural competence as the "cognitive, affective, and behavioral skills and characteristics that support effective and appropriate interaction in a variety of cultural contexts." These knowledge, attitude, and skill components of ICC have been demonstrated to be antecedent to intercultural effectiveness, typically operationalized in terms of general, work, social, and psychological adjustment in the host culture (Chen & Gabrenya, 2021). Intercultural learning (ICL), then, refers to the process by which individuals may improve their ICC and thus their effectiveness in an intercultural context (Haas, 2018).

Educators engaged in internationalization initiatives have looked to study abroad as an obvious pathway for facilitating students' ICC (Cushner, 2015). In general, study abroad refers to *credit mobility*, in which students study outside of their home country for a temporary period of time to earn credits that are recognized by their home institution, often driven by an interest in exploring unfamiliar cultures. This contrasts with *degree mobility*, in which students enroll in and complete a degree program outside of their home country, more commonly found in countries where educational institutions are of a quality or quantity that cannot meet students' needs (Kitsantas 2004; Wächter, 2014).

Study abroad has been described as a global phenomenon (Paige & Vande Berg, 2012), although its structure tends to vary somewhat by country and educational system (van der Poel, 2016). In comparison with data on degree-mobile students, there are significantly fewer sources of statistics on credit-mobile students globally (Nerlich, 2016). However, the available data indicate that participation in study abroad has increased dramatically in recent (pre-pandemic) years, fueled in part by a rise in short-term programs, defined as those lasting eight weeks or less (Chieffo & Griffiths, 2004; Donnelly-Smith, 2009). For example, during the 2018–19 academic year, nearly 470,000 students participated in the European Community Action Scheme for the Mobility of University Students programs (ERASMUS, 2020), an 8 percent increase over the previous year. During the same period, approximately 350,000 US students studied abroad, more than three times that of the number of participants two decades earlier (Institute of International Education, 2020). And over 58,000 students from universities in Australia studied abroad in 2019, an 11.3 percent increase over the previous year (Australian Government Department of Education, Skills, and Employment, 2021). Several nations where study abroad numbers have lagged behind expectations have put initiatives in place to increase participation. For example, the Japan Revitalization Strategy, Go Global Japan, and the Inter-University Exchange Project were implemented with the goal of increasing the number of Japanese students studying abroad from 60,000 in 2010 to approximately 120,000 by 2020 (Ota, 2018).

Nearly all study abroad programs, regardless of length, location, or disciplinary emphasis include the development of ICC as an implicitly or explicitly stated learning objective (Bloom & Miranda, 2015; Giovanangeli & Oguro, 2016; Lomicka & Ducate, 2021; Niehaus & Wegener, 2018). Yet the literature on study abroad has yielded a somewhat murky picture of the degree to which there has been success in achieving this outcome (Varela, 2017). This Element provides an overview and evaluation of the research on study abroad as a strategy for enhancing postsecondary students' ICC. The sections that follow discuss approaches to assessing intercultural competence in a study abroad context, detail the results of studies evaluating the efficacy of study abroad as a strategy for enhancing ICL, propose a theoretical framework for the mechanism underlying intercultural competence development via study abroad, and make recommendations for future directions in this area.

2 Assessing Intercultural Competence in Student Sojourners

Deardorff (2006) stated that intercultural competence is best assessed by multiple measures, combining both direct and indirect, as well as qualitative and quantitative, methods. Yet most research on study abroad–related ICC outcomes is based solely on self-report inventories, frequently the Intercultural Development Inventory or the Cross-Cultural Adaptability Inventory (Haas, 2018). Smaller-scale studies may use qualitative methods alone or in conjunction with standardized inventories. The sections that follow describe the quantitative and qualitative strategies most commonly implemented in studies assessing ICC in student sojourners.

2.1 Quantitative Methods

According to Deardorff (2015), there are over 100 different measures for assessing ICC. These instruments vary widely in terms of scope, theoretical and disciplinary underpinnings, constructs of interest, dimensionality, target population, presumed malleability of competencies, intended use, and psychometric properties. Those most commonly administered to student sojourners are detailed in Table 1.

2.2 Qualitative Methods

Qualitative methods of assessing study abroad–related ICC development generally focus on content analysis of interview transcripts as well as student writing, including journal entries (e.g., Johnson & Battalio, 2008; Opengart, 2018), responses to open-ended survey items and prompts (e.g., Jackson, 2015; Williams, 2009), blog and forum posts (Fukuda & Nishikawa Chávez, 2021; Jackson, 2015), and critical incidents (Tarchi et al., 2019). Student-generated photos have also been content analyzed (Williams, 2009). Coding schemes have utilized grounded theory approaches (e.g., Czerwionka et al., 2015; Mapp et al., 2007) and have been built around theoretical models of ICC, such as King and Baxter Magolda's (2005) concept of Intercultural Maturity (Opengart, 2018) and the Reflective Model of Intercultural Competence (Williams, 2009) as well as existing instruments, such as the Association of American Colleges & Universities' (AAC&U, 2009) Intercultural Knowledge and Competence VALUE Rubric (e.g., Fukuda & Nishikawa Chávez, 2021; Krishnan et al., 2021).

2.3 Methodological Concerns

Despite the availability of a wide range of quantitative and qualitative strategies for assessing student sojourners' ICC, the study abroad literature has been plagued by several serious methodological concerns. Reviews of ICC measures in general have raised questions about external validity (Matsumoto & Hwang, 2013) and cross-cultural measurement equivalence (Chen & Gabrenya, 2021).

Table 1 Quantitative measures of intercultural competence used in study abroad research

Measure	Author(s)	Target competency	Structure
Assessment of Intercultural Competence (AIC)	Fantini & Tirmizi (2006)	Intercultural competence defined as " … a complex of abilities needed to perform effectively and appropriately when interacting with others who are linguistically and culturally different from oneself" (Fantini & Tirmizi, 2006, p. 12)	54 items; 4 subscales: Knowledge, Attitudes, Skills, and Critical Awareness
Assessment of Intercultural Competence of Chinese College Students (AIC-CCS)	Wu et al., (2013)	Measures "specific ICC components such as tolerance, respect, harmony, sensitivity, and relationships, which are specifically related to traditional Chinese culture" (Peng et al., 2015, p. 147)	28 items; 6 factors: Knowledge of Self, Knowledge of Others, Attitudes, Intercultural Communication Skills, Intercultural Cognitive Skills, and Awareness
Cross-Cultural Adaptability Inventory (CCAI)	Kelley & Meyers (1995)	Effectiveness in intercultural interaction	50 items; 4 subscales: Emotional Resilience, Flexibility/Openness, Perceptual Acuity, and Personal Autonomy

Instrument	Citation	Description	Details
Cultural Intelligence Scale (CQ)	Ang et al. (2007)	Ability to function effectively in culturally diverse settings	20 items; 4 subscales: Metacognitive, Cognitive, Motivational, and Behavioral
Global Perspective Inventory (GPI)	Braskamp et al. (2013)	Students' perceptions of their own cultural heritage and how they relate to individuals from other cultures, backgrounds, and values	3 forms (general student, new student, study abroad posttest); 35 items; 3 dimensions, each with 2 subscales: Cognitive (Knowing and Knowledge scales), Intrapersonal (Identity and Affect scales), and Interpersonal (Social Responsibility and Social Interactions scales)
Global-Mindedness Scale	Hett (1993)	Globally interconnected worldview and sense of responsibility for members of the global community	30 items; 5 dimensions: Responsibility, Cultural Pluralism, Efficacy, Globalcentrism, and Interconnectedness
Intercultural Adjustment Potential Scale (ICAPS)	Matsumoto et al. (2011)	Intercultural adjustment potential	55 items; 4 subscales: Emotion Regulation, Openness, Flexibility, and Critical Thinking
Intercultural Development Inventory (IDI)	Hammer & Bennett (2002)	Stage of development in ability to shift cultural perspective and adapt to cultural differences and commonalities	50 items; 5 mindsets along continuum

Table 1 (cont.)

Measure	Author(s)	Target competency	Structure
Intercultural Effectiveness Scale (IES)	Kozai Group (2009)	Effectiveness in intercultural interaction	60 items; 3 subscales, each with 2 dimensions: Continuous Learning (Self-Awareness and Exploration scales), Interpersonal Engagement (Global Mindset and Relationship Interest scales), and Hardiness (Positive Regard and Resilience scales)
Intercultural Readiness Check (IRC)	van der Zee & Brinkmann (2004)	Intercultural competencies	63 items; 4 subscales: Intercultural Sensitivity, Intercultural Communication, Building Commitment, and Managing Uncertainty
Intercultural Sensitivity Index (ISI)	Olson & Kroeger (2001)	Affective component of intercultural communication competence. Based on Bennett's DMIS	49 items; 4 dimensions: Ethnocentrism, Ethnorelativism, Intercultural Communication Awareness, and Global Competency
Intercultural Sensitivity Inventory	Bhawuk & Brislin (1992)	Sensitivity to behaviors considered appropriate in individualist and collectivist cultures	46 items; 2 subscales: Individualism/ Collectivism, Flexibility/Open-Mindedness

Scale	Author(s)	Description	Items and subscales
Intercultural Sensitivity Scale (ISS)	Chen & Starosta (2000)	Measures the "ability to develop a positive emotion towards understanding and appreciating cultural differences that promotes appropriate and effective behavior in intercultural communication" (Chen & Starosta, 2000, p. 4)	44 items; 5 subscales: Interaction Engagement, Respect for Cultural Differences, Interaction Confidence, Interaction Enjoyment, and Interaction Attentiveness
Inventory for Cross-Cultural Sensitivity (Revised)	Cushner (1992)	Assesses "level of understanding and skill in relation to factors deemed important in successful cross-cultural interaction" (Mahon & Cushner, 2014, p. 487)	44 items; 4 subscales: Cultural Inclusion, Cultural Behavior, Cultural Anxiety, and Cognitive Flexibility
Miville-Guzman Universality-Diversity Scale (MGUDS)	Miville et al. (1999)	Awareness and acceptance of cultural similarities and differences	45 items (15-item short form); 3 subscales: Diversity of Contact, Relativistic Appreciation, and Comfort with Difference
Multicultural Personality Questionnaire (MPQ)	Van Der Zee & Van Oudenhoven (2000)	Traits relevant to intercultural success	78 items (40-item short form); 5 subscales: Cultural Empathy, Open-Mindedness, Emotional Stability, Flexibility, and Social Initiative

Table 1 (cont.)

Measure	Author(s)	Target competency	Structure
Perceived global awareness measure	Chieffo & Griffiths (2004)	Global awareness	27 items; 4 subscales: intercultural Awareness, Personal Growth and Development, Awareness of Global Interdependence, and Functional Knowledge of World Geography and Language
Sociocultural Adaptation Scale (SCAS)	Ward & Kennedy (1999)	Level of difficulty in tasks experienced by sojourners	Varying lengths; 2 dimensions: Cultural Empathy and Relatedness, Impersonal Endeavors, and Perils
Test to Measure Intercultural Competence (TMIC)	Schnabel et al. (2015)	Abilities that support handling challenging cross-cultural situations	75 self-report and 17 situational judgment items; (short form) 25 self-report and 6 situational judgment items
Wesleyan Intercultural Competence Scale (WICS)	Stemler et al. (2014)	Intercultural competence level based on Bennett's DMIS	Situational judgment test involving 16 situations US students might encounter during study abroad, each with 6 responses representing DMIS levels

Threats to the generalizability of research on study abroad outcomes in particular stem from an overreliance on cross-sectional evaluations of specific programs, typically attended by a small group of students from a single institution, most frequently in the USA (Ogden, 2015; Roy et al., 2019; Wolff & Borzikowsky, 2018). Some of the most consistent methodological limitations characterizing the study abroad literature involve the use of self-report instruments and nonequivalent control group designs, as well as a lack of cross-cultural inclusivity. These concerns are detailed in the following section.

2.3.1 Self-report

A significant concern with the use of self-report measures in study abroad research is social desirability bias. Kealey (2015, p. 14) observed that "most individuals in responding to questionnaire items will easily know the 'right answer', i.e. how to look culturally sensitive and knowledgeable." He suggested that this may be one reason why measures of ICC in general tend to have poor predictive validity. In addition to the potential for social desirability bias, the use of self-report measures may result in a form of underreporting one's own ICC that might be called the *intercultural learning paradox*. This is "the idea that as one gains ICC, they become more aware of their own intercultural insensitivity, discomfort with unfamiliar cultures, and need for cultural knowledge, and thus perceive themselves to be less interculturally skilled than at the beginning of their sojourn" (Goldstein, 2022, p. 33). This phenomenon may be exacerbated by students overestimating their level of ICC at the point of predeparture (Akdere et al., 2021; Iskhakova et al, 2021). The intercultural learning paradox is frequently offered as an explanation for research findings in which ICC scores fail to increase over the course of the sojourn, though it is also possible that such findings are due to a shift in reference group or may simply reflect what Acheson and Schneider-Bean (2019) refer to as the pendulum-like, nonlinear trajectory of ICC development. Additional research is needed to investigate the nature and extent of the intercultural learning paradox. Its existence, unless measured directly, would threaten the testability of hypotheses about the relation between level of intercultural experience and the development of ICC.

In addition to distortions due to social desirability bias and under- or over-reporting of one's own ICC, it may be that much of the relevant information about intercultural interactions is not accessible to the individual sojourner. Deardorff and Jones (2012) distinguished between the "effectiveness" and the "appropriateness" dimensions of ICC, indicating that whereas the former is the purview of the sojourner, the latter is dependent on the judgment and expectations of others within the host culture. Thus, Koester and Lustig (2015) suggested that questions of appropriateness, often included in assessments of ICC, may not be a valid area for self-report. Finally, an additional concern about the accessibility of one's own intercultural behavior comes from recent neuro-science studies, which indicate that some cultural differences may occur on a level that is beyond the individuals' conscious awareness (Chang, 2017).

Deardorff (2015) observed that ICC assessment strategies are beginning to shift from self-report inventories to direct, behavioral measures focusing on observable performance in real-life situations. Kealey (2015) asserted that this approach holds the greatest potential for measuring and predicting intercultural effectiveness. For example, Chi and Suthers (2015) implemented a relational strategy for assessing ICC based on a measure of social connectivity with members of the host community. These authors reason that it is not one's cultural knowledge in the absolute sense that results in effective intercultural interaction and adjustment, but one's ability to access relevant knowledge through relational networks. Ogden (2015) noted the need for greater attention to the effect of student mobility on the host community. Future research might explore the feasibility of measuring ICC in terms of host community impact in lieu of or to augment self-report data. Finally, Deardorff (2015) pointed out that the value of self-report measures of ICC is greatly dependent upon their intended use. For example, rather than predicting behavior in intercultural interactions, these instruments may be more useful as a tool for self-reflection and mentoring.

2.3.2 Nonequivalent Control Group Designs

The use of home campus control group comparisons has become more frequent as study abroad researchers have strived for greater methodological integrity. Yet it is well established that students who choose, or are able, to study abroad differ in meaningful ways from those who do not in terms of demographic characteristics (Kim & Lawrence, 2021; Salisbury et al., 2010), academic discipline (Contreras et al., 2019), personality traits (Ramirez, 2016), intergroup attitudes (Goldstein & Kim, 2006), language proficiency (Nowlan & Wang, 2018), and intercultural competence (Ramirez, 2016; Wickline et al., 2020; Zimmerman et al., 2020). Ogden (2015) suggested that these preexisting differences may exacerbate maturation effects, a threat to internal validity particularly relevant to study abroad research (Sutton et al, 2014). Ogden (p. 10) stated that "while a control group typically provides protection against this threat, students participating in education abroad programs are … already highly achieving, internationally oriented students. It would not be unreasonable, then, to assume their rate of development or growth would surpass that of the students in control groups." Salisbury et al. (2013) asserted that this selection effect may in fact be responsible for many of the research findings associating study abroad with ICC. Heinzmann et al. (2015) pointed out that even if the research design incorporates equivalent intervention and control groups, items on ICC outcome measures may not be equally meaningful to members of both groups. These issues of selection bias are not only relevant when making comparisons between those who do and do not study abroad, but also apply to comparisons across types of study abroad programs in that students' personality and intercultural attitudes vary with program type and preferred level of immersion across a number of program dimensions (e.g., duration, housing, language requirements; Goldstein, 2015, 2019; Zimmerman & Neyer, 2013).

Although it is generally impractical to randomly assign students to control and study abroad conditions, there are several strategies for improving the use of control groups in research on ICC. These include using a nonequivalent groups design involving the administration of a pretest-posttest to both groups to compare degree of change over time (e.g., Carley & Tudor, 2010), statistically controlling for confounding variables (Haas, 2018), constructing control groups matched on demographic variables and intercultural experience (e.g., Mule et al., 2018), and use of a waitlist control group consisting of future study abroad participants (e.g., Zimmerman et al., 2020).

2.3.3 Cross-cultural Inclusivity of Measures

The academic literature on ICC outcomes of study abroad has been based almost entirely on instruments developed in Europe and North America, creating the risk of an imposed etic when these instruments are administered to participants elsewhere. Although there exists a small number of locally constructed measures for use with non-English-speaking populations, such as Peng and Wu's (2016) intercultural contact scale for Chinese college students, a far more common approach is to use translated versions of English-language measures. With a few exceptions, such as Hammer's (2011) work on the IDI and van Oudenhoven et al.'s (2007) on the MPQ, there have been few efforts to attend to the cross-cultural equivalence of ICC instruments (Terzuolo, 2018). Furthermore, even if the cross-cultural generalizability of such instruments can be established, this does not rule out emic aspects of ICC, as have been identified in research on the cross-cultural universality of other phenomena, such as the Five-Factor Model. For example, in their discussion of the experiences of Chilean preservice teachers on short-term study abroad (STSA) programs, López and Morales (2021, p. 262) explained that "Chileans from the Global South are not accustomed to thinking of the world as revolving around them, as many students of the Global North studying abroad do . . . and instead are keenly aware of global issues from a position of less power, compared to the United States," thus illustrating potential cultural variability in the conceptualization of ICC.

In addition to concerns about cross-cultural equivalence, there has been little attention to participant identity in regard to ICC assessment. For example, items included in several measures of ICC, such as those addressing frequency of, or discomfort with, intercultural contact may be perceived differently by respondents from dominant majority racial/ethnic groups as compared with those from minoritized populations. Furthermore, Martin (2015) points to a failure to acknowledge that power dynamics are part of every intercultural encounter and that individuals from historically marginalized groups may never be viewed as competent, regardless of the knowledge and skills they demonstrate. Research such as Davidson's (2018) assessment of the measurement invariance of GPI items across racial/ethnic groups is warranted to allow for a better understanding of strategies to increase inclusivity. Study abroad scholars have identified the potential for cultural bias in measures of ICC as a significant conceptual, methodological, and ethical concern (e.g., Deardorff, 2008; Fukuda & Nishikawa Chávez, 2021; Hanada, 2019). Such bias may not only limit study abroad research from nonwestern institutions but may result in a failure to recognize how study abroad experiences and outcomes vary depending upon participants' diverse and intersectional identities. To address such concerns, Lieberman and Gamst (2015) advocated for greater application of the literature on multicultural competence and social justice to research on ICC.

3 Intercultural Competence Outcomes of Study Abroad

Given the methodological shortcomings of the study abroad literature discussed earlier and the difficulty of interpreting small, single-institution studies, this section will highlight the results of meta-analyses, systematic literature reviews, multi-institution studies, and single-institution, multi-program research on study abroad outcomes. Single-institution studies are addressed in the section that follows in regard to the specific participant and program characteristics associated with gains in ICC.

3.1 Meta-analyses

The association between study abroad and favorable ICC outcomes is supported by four separate meta-analytical studies evaluating study abroad experiences of one year or less, each with a wide range of outcome variables. Burrow (2019) analyzed 72 studies (85 effect sizes) with pre-post designs. Haas (2018) investigated 28 studies (35 effect sizes) and Varela (2017) assessed 30 studies (38 effect sizes), both targeting within-subjects, pre-post designs, or between-subjects comparisons with a nonstudy abroad control group. The results of all three meta-analyses indicated that study abroad was associated with gains in ICC. Varela found the largest effect sizes for cognitive, followed by affective and then behavioral outcomes. Zhang and Zhou (2019) conducted a meta-analysis of 31 studies on a variety of interventions designed to promote aspects of ICC. They found that studying or working abroad had a greater effect than culture-based teaching materials, classroom activities, or integrated intercultural programs, such as intercultural courses or training.

3.2 Systematic Literature Reviews

Two systematic literature reviews on this topic support the efficacy of study abroad for enhancing ICC. Roy et al. (2019) investigated 75 studies for a variety of outcomes (cultural, personal, and career) for participants in study abroad programs of one year or less. In terms of cultural outcomes, these authors reported that study abroad was associated with increased cultural awareness and adaptability, global mindedness, and some forms of cultural intelligence, with mixed results on cultural sensitivity and empathy. An additional review, discussed in greater detail later in this Element, indicated that overall, even short-term programs of eight weeks or less produce gains in some forms of ICC (Goldstein, 2022).

3.3 Multi-institution Studies

Perhaps the best known and most comprehensive multi-institution study is the Georgetown Consortium Research Project (Vande Berg et al., 2009), in which nearly 1,300 students from 190 US universities were surveyed at three points in time (pre-post and five-month delayed posttest) using the IDI as well as a language proficiency measure. The students were either enrolled in a domestic institution (the control group) or were attending one of 61 study abroad programs, which varied widely in duration, structure, and content. This study was instrumental in challenging the "immersion assumption" – the idea that intercultural contact alone enhances student sojourners' ICC (Vande Berg et al., 2012). The Georgetown Consortium Project also established the importance of deliberate intervention in that although study abroad participants had significantly greater gains in IDI than the control students, the IDI scores of those in programs with a mentoring component far exceeded that of other participants. Hanada (2019) investigated ICC outcomes for 303 Japanese students from 13 universities attending programs of varying lengths in Canada and the USA. A back-translated Japanese language version of the IDI was administered in a pre-post design and indicated a small increase in scores. Specific predictor variables incorporated into the design of these two studies are discussed in subsequent sections of this Element.

Multi-institution studies by Salisbury et al. (2013) and Zimmerman et al. (2020) used two different designs to address concerns about selection bias in research on study abroad and ICC. Salisbury et al. statistically adjusted for selection bias using demographic-, experience-, and intercultural competence-based pretest indices for 1,647 students from 17 US undergraduate institutions who were surveyed at the beginning and end of their first year and at the end of their final year in college. While scores on the Miville-Guzman Universality Diversity Scale indicated that study abroad was associated with significant gains on the Diversity of Contact subscale, which assesses engagement in diverse social and cultural activities, study abroad was no more beneficial in terms of other aspects of ICC (Relativistic Appreciation and Comfort with Difference) than on-campus experiences and in fact may have been less so. Zimmerman et al. (2020) addressed selection bias using a pre-post waitlist control design. A total of 3,070 students at Erasmus-participating German universities were designated as members of either a control group of students with no intention to study abroad, a control group of future study abroad participants, or as recent participants. Students who had experienced study abroad outscored members of the other two groups on multicultural self-efficacy and metacognitive intercultural competence and had significantly lower scores on a measure of intergroup anxiety.

Stebleton et al. (2013) compared outcomes of participants in five different international experiences, including own institution study abroad, other institution study abroad, international service learning, informal educational travel, and recreational travel. Nearly 100,000 undergraduate students from twelve large, public universities in the USA responded to a comprehensive survey which included items about international experiences and self-reported gains in understanding "the complexities of global issues, ability to apply disciplinary knowledge in a global context, linguistic or cultural competency in another language, ability to work with people from other cultures, and comfort working with people from other cultures" (p. 2). In general, participating in study abroad either through one's own or another institution was associated with greater gains on the ICC items as compared with the other international travel experiences. Finally, Nguyen (2017) administered the Intercultural Effectiveness Scale using a pre-post-three-month delayed post design to 55 students who attended eight different STSA programs sponsored by three Texas institutions. The results indicated significant gains in intercultural competence, which was driven by increases on three of the six subscales (Self-Awareness, Global Mindset, and Relationship Interest).

3.4 Single-Institution, Multi-Program Studies

Several US studies have focused on the outcomes of multiple faculty-led programs originating from a single institution. Kartoshkina et al. (2013) investigated the ICC development of 967 University of Delaware students on 46 different STSA programs using an internally designed pre-post instrument. Paired-samples *t*-tests indicated significant growth in students' self-reported knowledge of the host culture and cross-cultural awareness and adaptation. Chieffo and Griffiths (2004) compared the ICC gains of 1,509 University of Delaware students on 71 different STSA programs with a home campus control group of 847 students enrolled in courses similar to those offered abroad. STSA participants scored significantly higher than the control students on the intercultural awareness, personal growth and development, and functional knowledge subscales of the authors' self-designed measure of global awareness, though no significant differences were found for awareness of global interdependence. Using the same global awareness measure in a two times pre-post design (before and after predeparture training and post-sojourn), Kurt et al. (2013) surveyed 1,178 students from Elon University in North Carolina who were enrolled in one of 23 separate STSA programs. Significant increases in global awareness occurred between the second and third survey administrations, indicating that the intercultural preparation alone was not sufficient to increase ICC. In a study designed to focus on the specific program components associated with ICC gains (and detailed in subsequent sections of this Element), Whatley et al. (2021) reported small but statistically significant pre-post differences in the GPI scores of over 2,000 participants in faculty-led STSA programs offered by a large research university in the Southeast USA. Finally, significant pre-post gains were found on all four subscales of the Cross-Cultural Adaptability Inventory (CCAI) administered to 87 students from a small Pennsylvania college who had participated in one or more STSA programs in five different countries (Mapp, 2012).

3.5 Long-term Outcome Studies

It is important to distinguish those longitudinal designs that involve pre-post assessments within the confines of the program duration from those in which assessments were administered after the program's completion date. There have been increased calls for this latter form of longitudinal research, along with the recognition that there may be a delay between the student's experience and the manifestation of intercultural growth (Pilon, 2017). For example, Gower et al. (2019) reported that whereas Australian nursing students showed significant decreases in self-assessed cultural skills and awareness immediately following two- to four-week placements in Tanzania, Cambodia, Thailand, India, or the Philippines, significant increases were observed in their scores when assessed one year out.

Additional evidence for the long-term effects of study abroad come from surveys of study abroad alumni investigating the maintenance of intercultural learning over time. In a much-cited large survey of Institute for the International Education of Students alumni from five decades, the majority of respondents indicated that their experience abroad continued to shape their worldview and interest in intercultural learning (Dwyer, 2004). Paige et al. (2009) surveyed, and interviewed a subsample of, alumni from 22 different US institutions who had participated in study abroad over several decades. Overall, respondents indicated that their study abroad experiences significantly impacted their global engagement, subsequent education, and career paths. Dukes et al. (1994) surveyed Semester at Sea participants ten years post-sojourn and reported that they were able to maintain a global perspective and that the experience contributed to positive personal growth. Multiple surveys of single program alumni, including STSA participants, also show sustained gains in intercultural development when tested up to several years post-sojourn (e.g., Berg & Schwander, 2019). Yet, in his research agenda for US education abroad, Ogden (2015, p. 5) pointed out that "Although informative, the utility of such longitudinal studies is weakened by their having mostly utilized student self-reporting methodologies and failing to position their findings relative to comparison or control groups."

There are a number of studies using a pre-post and delayed posttest design that address this methodological concern, including STSA studies (e.g., Anderson et al., 2006; Gower et al., 2019; Rexeisen et al., 2008) which demonstrate intercultural gains sustained for several weeks to a year post-return. The Wabash National Study of Liberal Arts Education, for example, assessed the effect of "high impact practices" (Kuh, 2008) including study abroad in a survey administered to students from 17 institutions in different regions of the USA during their first college year and then again four years later (Kilgo et al., 2015). Study abroad was found to be a significant, positive predictor of intercultural effectiveness at year four, as measured by both the Miville-Guzman Universality-Diversity Scale and the Openness to Diversity/ Challenge measure.

Future longitudinal research may produce a more nuanced picture of study abroad–related intercultural learning. For example, there is evidence that some aspects of ICC may be sustained or even increase over time whereas others may decrease. Nguyen (2017) administered the IES to STSA participants from three Texas institutions before, after, and at three months post-sojourn. Scores on the Global Mindset subscale, which assesses interest in different cultures, while still significantly higher than predeparture levels, had declined at the three-month point. Yet Relationship Interest scores, which indicate willingness to maintain intercultural relationships, did not show significant gains until three months after the program.

These outcome assessments provide general support for study abroad as a viable strategy for enhancing students' ICC. Heinzmann et al. (2015) argued that the fact that positive outcomes have resulted from investigations based on a wide range of experiences and measures only strengthens this conclusion. Yet these general results provide little guidance for student advising, predeparture orientation, and program design. The sections that follow detail specific factors that facilitate or inhibit growth in ICC during study abroad and may contribute to the development of best practices for the design of study abroad programs.

4 Facilitating and Inhibiting Factors

As it has become clear that intercultural contact alone does not result in the development of ICC (Vande Berg et al., 2012), there has been a growing call for research on study abroad to shift focus to the specific participant and program design factors that affect learning outcomes (Engberg & Jourian, 2015; Hofer et al., 2016). Study abroad program design has become increasingly elaborate in an attempt to incorporate features that produce intercultural learning. For example, Iskhakova et al. (2021, p. 6) described the multiple components of a two-week immersion experience for Australian global business students, which, in addition to a semester-long series of predeparture activities, included the following:

> a series of academic seminars at a partner institution, corporate site visits, panel discussions with managers, entrepreneurs, government officials, interactions, socialisations with local nationals and student ambassadors, visits to culturally significant sites, self-guided exploration activities, reflective and feedback sessions, and other culturally immersive activities. Students were also required to maintain a regular journal of learning during the tour. The post-study tour stage consisted of working on an individual learning report and post-tour seminar with reflection and programme closure.

Yet the degree of variability across programs, the difficulty of isolating the effects of critical components within programs, and minimal reporting of program and participant characteristics make identifying facilitating and inhibiting factors challenging. The sections that follow describe patterns that have emerged in participant and program characteristics associated with growth in students' ICC.

4.1 Participant Characteristics

Several study abroad researchers have called for greater attention to sojourners' individual differences and the role of person-situation fit in shaping study abroad outcomes (e.g., Goldoni, 2015; Li et al., 2013; Roy et al., 2019). The following sections discuss the role of participants' gender, racial/ethnic and cultural identity, personality traits and beliefs, language proficiency, previous travel experience and intercultural knowledge, and acculturation strategy on ICC development.

4.1.1 Gender

Studies from Australia, Europe, and the USA overwhelmingly report more female than male participants in study abroad (Van Mol, 2022). Several explanations have been provided for this gender gap. Women tend to study subject areas, such as social sciences, humanities, and the arts, which offer more opportunities to study abroad (Cordue & Netz, 2021; Di Pietro, 2021) and greater flexibility for doing so, thus reducing the risk of delayed graduation (Goldstein & Kim, 2006). Women also tend to outperform men academically, which may better position them for study abroad programs or scholarships based on academic merit (Di Pietro, 2021). In addition, female students are more likely to cite gaining intercultural experience (Tompkins et al., 2017) or interest in exploring other cultures (Van Mol, 2022) as a reason for studying abroad and to have positive expectations of study abroad, expectations which are associated with significantly less ethnocentrism and intercultural communication apprehension and greater language interest as compared with male students (Kim & Goldstein, 2005).

Despite concerns about the gender gap in study abroad participation, few studies have systematically investigated gender differences in the development of ICC once abroad. Those that have generally report either that sojourning women outscore men on measures of ICC or a lack of significant gender differences. One of the largest of these is the Georgetown Consortium study, in which pre-post IDI assessment indicated that whereas female students as a group made significant gains, male students did no better than the on-campus control group, and in fact decreased in IDI scores while abroad. Terzuolo (2018) also reported that female students were significantly more likely than male students to show positive changes in IDI scores while studying abroad. In addition, DeJordy et al. (2020) reported that women outscored men on a qualitative assessment of a reflection task. Finally, using a posttest only design, Tompkins et al. (2017) reported statistically significant gender differences on the Intercultural Sensitivity Scale (ISS; Chen & Starosta, 2000) for US students; while women who studied abroad scored significantly higher on the Interaction Attentiveness subscale than women who had not studied abroad, the ISS scores of men who studied abroad did not differ significantly from those who did not. In contrast, several studies reported that gender was not a significant predictor of ICC outcomes while abroad (Demetry & Vaz, 2017; Hanada, 2019; Kehl & Morris, 2008; Makara & Canon, 2020; Rexeisen et al., 2008). None of the studies reviewed for this Element reported that men outscored women on any measure of ICC.

4.1.2 Racial/Ethnic and Cultural Identity

Despite considerable attention among scholars and practitioners in recent decades to the lack of diversity among study abroad participants, few investigations of study abroad outcomes have included analyses based on the participants' racial/ethnic, or cultural identification. In one study of STSA, Nguyen et al. (2018) compared US monocultural participants with multicultural participants, defined as individuals identifying with more than one culture, including "immigrants, refugees, indigenous people, racial/ethnic minorities, multiracial individuals, those in interracial relationships, and third-culture kids" (p. 121). They reported qualitative analysis of interview data which indicated that while multicultural participants believed that the study abroad experience had facilitated their personal and ICC development, this was often enmeshed with experiences of marginalization and lack of belonging. Furthermore, the monocultural, but not multicultural, participants grew in self-efficacy and cultural intelligence (CQ) over the course of the sojourn. The authors noted that the multicultural participants started their sojourns with higher CQ scores and had thus "already acquired the behavioral, cognitive, and metacognitive skills of learning, navigating, and negotiating cultures before going abroad" (p. 126). Similarly, Engberg and Jourian (2015, p. 2), reported that Students of Color scored significantly higher than White students on a predeparture measure of intercultural wonderment, which "is manifested as students intentionally push themselves outside their comfort zones, feel immersed in the culture of the host country, explore new habits and behaviors while abroad, and interact with individuals from the host country outside the classroom" and Stebleton et al. (2013) analyzed survey data from over 287,000 students at 12 large public universities in the USA and found that underrepresented minority students reported greater gains on a number of outcomes including linguistic/cultural competency and understanding the complexity of global issues, although not in comfort working with people from other cultures.

In a study which focused on White and Latinx US students on four different short-term programs, Opengart (2018) applied King and Baxter Magolda's (2005) Intercultural Maturity framework to the analysis of student writing and found that although both groups demonstrated growth in ICC, and there were few differences between White and Latinx students' journals, the Latinx students made more comments regarding cultural comparisons, which the author suggested may indicate greater openness to multiple perspectives. Clearly, additional research targeting the role of racial/ethnic identity in the development of ICC abroad is needed to interpret these findings. Yet it seems evident that the intercultural knowledge and experience that accompanies minoritized identities (discussed further in Section 4.1.5) should not be overlooked in conceptualizing and assessing ICC.

In terms of cultural identity and nationality, Tarchi et al. (2019) compared the study abroad outcomes of US students and European Erasmus Mundus students on programs in Italy and found that Erasmus Mundus students expressed greater intercultural sensitivity than the US students as indicated by DMIS-based analysis of qualitative data from video logs. US study abroad students' narratives were generally judged to be more ethnocentric, whereas Erasmus Mundus students' were more ethnorelative. Tarchi et al. attributed these findings to several factors, including the greater cultural insularity of the US students, who scored higher on identification with conationals, and the fact that many of the Erasmus students experienced two different forms of cross-cultural /linguistic encounters by taking classes in Italy that were taught in English. Douglas and Jones-Rikkers (2001) suggested that US students generally have more to gain from a study abroad experience than students from other countries due to their tendency to assume that other cultures should conform to American customs. Similarly, Uhlmann (2012, p. 381) coined the term *American psychological isolationism* to refer to "a distinctive cultural mindset characterized by a lack of regard for and even lack of awareness of the perspectives of other countries, coupled with a passionate desire to spread American values throughout the world."

It appears that many US sojourners are aware of these negative perceptions and find exposure to stereotypes that target their American identity to be a significant source of stress (Goldstein, 2017a). Thus, it is possible that the intercultural growth of US study abroad participants may be impeded to some extent by stereotype threat, which occurs when one expects to be judged negatively based on stereotypes of one's social group and when one feels at risk of confirming those stereotypes. For example, stereotype threat was reported by US students abroad in a study conducted just prior to and following the 2016 presidential election of Donald Trump (Goldstein, 2017a). Thus, there is reason to expect that ICC development may vary to some extent with the nature and strength of national identity. Additional research may lead to a better understanding of the relation between national identity and study abroad outcomes.

4.1.3 Personality Traits and Beliefs

Based on an understanding that there exist consistent individual differences in response to cross-cultural experiences (Ramirez, 2016), multiple studies have investigated the relation between personality traits and ICC in students as well as other sojourner populations. Many of these studies have focused on the Five-Factor Model (e.g., Openness to Experience, Conscientiousness, Extraversion, Agreeableness, and Neuroticism), whereas others utilize measures of specific traits perceived to be directly relevant to intercultural interaction. Studies of student sojourners from a wide range of backgrounds point to Five-Factor Model Openness to Experience and Extraversion as key predictors of the development of ICC (e.g., Burke et al., 2009; Harrison, 2012; Ramirez, 2016; Rings & Allehyani, 2020; Wang & Ching, 2015). For example, in their meta-analysis of correlates of cultural competence as assessed by the Sociocultural Adaptation Scale, Wilson et al. (2013) found that for Five-Factor Model personality traits, the largest effect sizes were for Openness and Extraversion. Although the 66 studies they analyzed included a variety of sojourner populations, more than half of the participants were international students. Ramirez (2016, p. 92) suggested that "students who are high in openness … have less rigid views of right and wrong, best and worse, appropriate and inappropriate, consequently adapting their behavior more easily to novel situations in cultural diverse setting." Deardorff (2006) also included openness among "requisite attitudes" for the development of ICC in her model along with respect (valuing other cultures and diversity) and curiosity and discovery (tolerance of ambiguity and uncertainty). The Adventurousness facet of Openness may be particularly relevant to the development of ICC in that it is associated with a preference for greater immersion on a variety of program components (i.e., duration, program model, and housing; Goldstein, 2019).

Extraversion is also considered facilitative of intercultural interaction and thus the ability to attain more immersive experiences (Ramirez, 2016). Neuroticism (i.e., low emotional stability) tends to be negatively correlated with ICC (Lee et al., 2010; Rings & Allehyani, 2020; Wang & Ching, 2015;

Wilson et al., 2013) and possible associations between ICC and Conscientiousness and Agreeableness are less clear. Taking an interactionist approach, Geeraert et al. (2019) reported that although students from loose cultures sojourning to tight cultures have more difficulty than the reverse, those scoring higher on Agreeableness and Honesty-Humility were better able to adjust to a context with strong behavioral norms.

Van der Zee and Van Oudenhoven (2013) suggested that the traits relevant to the development of ICC are those associated with the tendency to perceive an intercultural situation as a challenge rather than a threat. Based on Ward et al.'s (2001) A (Affect), B (Behavior), C (Cognition) model of culture shock, Van der Zee and Van Oudenhoven argued that these include traits central to coping with stress (e.g., emotional stability, flexibility) as well as social-perceptual traits (e.g., social initiative, cultural empathy, open-mindedness), which facilitate cultural learning. Several studies using the MPQ to assess these traits support the predictive validity of this model among student sojourners (e.g., Leong, 2007; Mol, Van Oudenhoven, & Van der Zee, 2001; Van Oudenhoven & Van der Zee, 2002). Chao et al. (2017) demonstrated the importance of implicit cultural beliefs for the adjustment of student sojourners enrolled in an exchange program in Hong Kong. Those who viewed cultural attributes as more fixed (versus malleable) experienced greater intercultural rejection sensitivity, which then affected cross-cultural adjustment (general, social, and academic) and subsequent CQ scores.

4.1.4 Language Proficiency

Schnabel et al. (2015) included willingness to use a foreign language as a feature of their model of intercultural competence. Language proficiency is assumed to facilitate access to immersive experiences (Wilson et al., 2013) and reduce the likelihood of uncomfortable or awkward intercultural interactions (Tsang, 2022). In fact, research has demonstrated that language and communication competence is associated with greater host-culture contact (Ward & Kennedy, 1993; Wilson et al., 2013), more effective intercultural interactions (Chen & Starosta, 1996; Masgoret & Ward, 2006; Sercu, 2002; Wilson et al., 2013), and increased intercultural sensitivity (Olson & Kroeger, 2001). Among student sojourners, language proficiency has consistently been associated with cross-cultural adjustment. For example, Yu et al. (2019) found that for international students in Hong Kong from diverse nationalities, English-language proficiency was a significant predictor of psychological adaptation and both English and Cantonese language proficiency were significant predictors of sociocultural adaptation.

Empirical research on the role of language proficiency in the development of ICC among student sojourners has generally involved including language proficiency as one of several predictor variables (Tsang, 2022). For example, Hanada (2019) reported prior English-language proficiency to be a predictor of IDI change scores among Japanese students studying in Canada and the USA. Vande Berg et al. (2009) reported that in the Georgetown Consortium study, students who had previously taken language courses in high school and college had significantly greater gains in intercultural competence as measured by the IDI as compared with those who had not. In addition, Ramirez (2016) reported second-language proficiency to be a significant predictor of CQ scores among international students at four universities in Colombia. Yet support for the importance of language proficiency in the development of ICC has not been unequivocal. Pedersen (2010) and Spenader and Retka (2015) reported that second-language ability had no significant impact on intercultural competence as measured by the IDI. Further, Bloom and Miranda (2015) found language ability to be unrelated to scores on the Intercultural Sensitivity Index.

Beyond language proficiency per se and the accompanying access to the host culture, it may be that language-related attitudes also play a role in ICC. Interest in language learning may be part of a more global receptivity to intercultural interaction in that it is a predictor of participation in study abroad (Goldstein & Kim, 2006) as well as of the preference for more immersive study abroad programs (Goldstein, 2015). Iqbal (2019) found that bilingual students demonstrated greater cultural growth than monolingual students in Japan, where the language was unfamiliar, and suggested that language proficiency, even if not relevant to the host country, is associated with decreased fear of language barriers. In addition, in terms of having the confidence to initiate or engage in intercultural interactions, the student's self-perceived language competence, which is distinct from objective language proficiency (Redmond & Bunyi, 1991), may be more critical. For example, language confidence has been identified as a predictor of willingness to communicate across cultures (Yashima, Zenuk-Nishide, & Shimizu, 2004) and of student sojourners' sociocultural adaptation (Yu & Shen, 2012). Finally, the student's language ability and attitudes may interact with host-culture linguistic conditions. For example, based on qualitative analysis of interview data, Nguyen et al. (2018) identified specific language-related experiences abroad that affected students' perceptions of culture, including being in the racial majority but linguistic minority, being in the linguistic majority but racial minority, or hearing about these experiences from others. Greater clarity may emerge from more complex investigations of the role of language proficiency in the development of ICC which consider the relation between language proficiency, language of instruction, and the language-related conditions of the host culture.

4.1.5 Previous Intercultural Experience

Several studies suggest that previous intercultural experience and knowledge may not provide an advantage in terms of intercultural learning (e.g., Behrnd & Porzelt, 2012; Bloom & Miranda, 2015; Coker et al., 2018; Engle & Crowne, 2014; Hanada, 2019; Ramirez, 2016). In fact, some studies suggest the opposite (e.g., Gondra & Czerwionka, 2018; Vande Berg et al., 2009; Zimmerman et al., 2020), with greater increases in ICC for sojourners with a moderate level of international experience (Iskhakova et al. 2021, p. 11) or for those who were initially less interculturally experienced or knowledgeable – what McKeown (2009) labeled the "first time effect." One explanation for this finding is that experienced sojourners may start out with greater levels of ICC than their peers (Hudson & Morgan, 2020; Pedersen, 2010; Zimmerman et al., 2020) suggesting a ceiling effect for these individuals. In addition, more experienced sojourners may self-assess as lower on measures of ICC than novice sojourners (e.g., Bloom & Miranda, 2015), due, perhaps, to the aforementioned intercultural learning paradox. As Bloom and Miranda (2015, p. 577) observed "the group with less experience interculturally did not have enough intercultural awareness to realize that they had more to learn … whereas the group with more intercultural experience had enough understanding to realize that they could be yet more interculturally sensitive."

Inconsistencies in the literature on previous intercultural experience may be due in part to variation in the labeling and operationalization of terms as well as whether ICC is assessed on a culture-general or culture-specific level. Ott and Iskhakova (2019) conducted a systematic review of definitions of "international experience" in studies focusing on the development of cultural intelligence and found that international experience has been labeled (e.g., cross-cultural exposure, multicultural interactions, international travel) and assessed (e.g., frequency or duration of travel, number of countries visited, having friends or partners from other cultures, attending cultural events, language proficiency) in a wide variety of ways. In addition, the majority of studies finding greater ICC development among those with little or no previous intercultural experience tend to have conceptualized ICC on a culture-general level. Studies show that experienced sojourners, who start out with high levels of ICC, may be better able to develop culture-specific knowledge of their host culture and the associated culturally appropriate behaviors. For example, Kurt et al. (2013) found that previous travel experience may facilitate the development of students' functional knowledge, such as knowing how to make a phone call to someone in a different country or knowledge of currency conversion rates.

Future investigations of the relation between previous intercultural experience or knowledge and ICC might consider the experiences of individuals at advanced levels of intercultural learning, who have been largely excluded from the student mobility literature. For example, Messelink and Ten Thije (2012) studied members of a cohort they identified as "Erasmus Generation 2.0." These students, enrolled in internships at European organizations, had extensive previous travel experiences and had mastered at least two languages other than their native language. Based on qualitative analysis of multiple dinner conversations, these authors identified several features of the students' discourse which demonstrated a sophisticated and flexible facility with cultural and linguistic knowledge, including the ability to assume an outsider perspective on their own culture and to identify similarities and find unity across cultural boundaries. Future research might also explore whether and how prior intercultural experience may interact with location. Iqbal (2019) compared short-term programs in two different countries – Japan and India – and found that perceived cultural learning was greater in Japan for students with more intercultural experience and in India for less experienced participants. Iqbal attributed the intercultural learning of less experienced sojourners in India to fewer linguistic challenges and a more structured learning environment. Finally, it may be useful to expand the definition of intercultural experience to include knowledge gained from interactions across groups that are not international in nature. Specifically, the same skills that individuals develop from negotiating interactions based on minoritized identities may be applicable to a study abroad context. For example, Lu et al. (2015) reported that Black students studying in China drew on the ability to code switch to facilitate intercultural interaction. Volpone et al. (2018) found an association between the number of minority statuses experienced by international students in their home country and adjustment to the host culture.

4.1.6 Acculturation Strategy

Some studies have applied Berry's (2003) acculturation model to the adjustment of student sojourners. Berry's general framework identifies four strategies based on two dimensions: the degree to which the acculturating individual (1) values maintenance of heritage culture and identity, and (2) values establishing relationships within the host society. Individuals who seek to both maintain their heritage culture and establish relationships within the host society use an integration strategy. Those who seek to maintain their heritage culture without establishing relationships with host-culture members use a separation strategy, whereas those in the reverse situation (establishing relationships with host-culture members without maintaining one's heritage culture) use an assimilation strategy. Individuals who withdraw from both their heritage and host cultures use a marginalization strategy. Berry's model indicates that the selection of strategy is not the individual's alone but interacts with the acculturation expectations of the dominant groups, which vary along the same two dimensions depending upon the inclusivity of the host culture. Berry (2019) explained that an integration strategy is only possible when the dominant culture meets certain conditions, including low levels of prejudice and ethnocentrism.

Applications of this model to study abroad students find that acculturation strategies oriented toward the host culture are associated with better outcomes than are those oriented toward the home culture (Demes & Geeraert, 2014; Pedersen, 2010). Nguyen (2013) noted that acculturation strategies may differ depending on the domain, such as language use, social networks, daily living habits, cultural traditions, communication style, family socialization, and cultural knowledge. Using the Acculturation Index (Ward & Rana-Deuba, 1999), which assesses acculturation strategies in such areas, Tarchi et al. (2019) suggested that the higher levels of ICC development they observed in European as opposed to US students abroad may be due to the latter group's less integrative acculturation strategy, manifested by greater identification with conationals.

Also relevant to study abroad students' acculturation strategies are recent studies investigating students' online, phone, and texting connections to home culture friends and family, given that at least among US participants, students abroad communicate with friends and family at approximately the same frequency as do students when on their home campus (Hofer et al., 2016). For example, Engle and Engle (2012) reported a decrease in ICC as measured by the IDI when they lifted restrictions on students' email and Internet use. Researchers might consider the degree to which these forms of communication with home culture members may be indicative of an integration or separation acculturation strategy.

4.2 Program Characteristics

In addition to a closer analysis of participant features, recent research on student mobility has increasingly attended to the specific program characteristics associated with favorable ICC outcomes in an effort to identify best practices in program design. Contributing to this shift may be the growth of faculty-led STSA, which allows for greater flexibility in program components. Research of this type is supported by the model put forth by Engle and Engle (2003) detailing levels of immersion across multiple program characteristics (e.g., duration, housing, language of instruction). The sections that follow discuss the extant research on the relation between ICC development and program duration, predeparture interventions, program model, housing, language of instruction, internship/service activities, program location, and pedagogical features.

4.2.1 Duration

Much research has investigated the role of sojourn duration in achieving ICC and related outcomes. This issue has gained importance in recent years as STSA has become increasingly popular among sending institutions across the globe (e.g., Erasmus, 2021; Institute of International Education, 2020; International Education Association of Australia, 2016; Shimmi & Ota, 2018). In the USA, short-term programs of eight weeks or less have become the dominant form of student mobility (Institute of International Education, 2020). Identifying the relation between program duration and ICC is complicated by the variability among programs of similar duration in terms of other program features. However, some fairly consistent patterns have emerged. This section discusses the effectiveness of short-term experiences in developing ICC and examines whether longer programs do indeed yield more favorable outcomes.

Chiocca (2021, p. 36) observed that "short-term programs have been under scrutiny in the past decade, as scholars question whether growth (linguistic and intercultural) can be achieved in short stays abroad (Chieffo & Griffiths, 2004; Dwyer, 2004), with a tacit assumption that limited duration is synonymous with superficiality." A systematic review of 68 studies of STSA program outcomes indicated that, although there were some cases where these programs were found to have no or a limited effect on ICC (e.g., Anderson et al., 2006; Davies et al., 2015; Demetry & Vaz, 2017; Kehl & Morris, 2008), overall, STSA appears to enhance students' intercultural interest, knowledge, and awareness with more limited affective and behavioral outcomes (Goldstein, 2022). Studies of varying n-sizes, using a wide variety of qualitative and quantitative measures have reported positive ICC outcomes for students on STSA programs (e.g., Bretag & van der Veen, 2017; Capps et al., 2018; Chieffo & Griffiths, 2004; Czerwionka et al., 2015; Fukuda & Nishikawa Chávez, 2021; Gaia, 2015; Gondra & Czerwionka, 2018; Gower et al., 2019; Granel et al., 2021; Gullekson et al., 2011; Harris et al., 2019; Kartoshkina et al., 2013; Kurt et al., 2013; Lomicka & Ducate, 2021; Lo-Philip et al., 2015; Lumkes et al., 2012; Malewski et al., 2012; Nguyen, 2017; Roberts et al., 2019; Shiveley & Misco, 2015; Smith & Yang, 2017; Torii et al., 2020; Whatley et al., 2021), including a decrease in stereotyped perceptions of members of the host culture as compared with pre-sojourn measures (Carley & Tutor, 2010; Makara & Canon, 2020) as well an increased likelihood of subsequent travel or international study (Dwyer, 2004; Kato & Suzuki, 2019; Lewis & Niesenbaum, 2005; Mapp et al., 2007). There is no clear pattern among STSA programs in terms of the ideal program length. Whatley et al. (2021) investigated the effect of duration among STSA programs that ranged from two to seven weeks on GPI scores and found that duration was not a significant predictor of outcomes.

Studies comparing STSA with longer programs generally support Dwyer's (2004) contention that "more is better" (e.g., Dwyer, 2004; Kehl & Morris, 2008; Strange & Gibson, 2020). For example, Coker et al. (2018) compared US students who participated in no study abroad, one STSA program, two STSA programs, semester-long study abroad, and semester plus STSA on items from the National Survey of Student Engagement, such as the frequency with which they subsequently included diverse perspectives in discussions and assignments. These findings indicated that while STSA was of some value beyond that of not studying abroad at all, participating in multiple STSA experiences did not approach the benefits of a single, semester-long program. Those who participated in semester programs outscored the other groups, with no clear benefit for an additional STSA experience.

Some of the strongest evidence for the effect of duration comes from studies with a pre-post design since students with higher levels of ICC may self-select into more immersive mobility experiences (Goldstein, 2015). Several of these studies compared STSA to semester- or year-long programs. In general, the ICC outcomes of longer programs were superior to that of STSA (e.g., Behrnd & Porzelt, 2012; Ingraham & Peterson, 2004; Medina-López-Portillo, 2004; Pedersen, 2009; Vande Berg et al., 2009). For example, IDI scores in the Georgetown Study (Vande Berg et al., 2009) indicated that participants in the shortest program (thirteen to eighteen weeks) actually decreased in intercultural sensitivity, whereas members of the longer (nineteen to twenty-five weeks and twenty-five weeks to a year) demonstrated gains. Medina-López-Portillo (2004) compared a seven-week (STSA) Taxco program with a sixteen-week Mexico City program on participants' qualitative data and IDI scores and found that those in the longer program were more than twice as likely as the STSA participants to advance to the next DMIS stage. Although most investigations of study abroad duration found that longer programs were associated with greater gains in ICC, some indicated a lack of additional ICC development beyond that achieved in a semester or medium-length program (e.g., Heinzmann et al., 2015; Vande Berg et al., 2009).

Advocates of longer study abroad programs suggest that duration is a proxy for level of immersion. For example, Strange and Gibson (2020,

p. 86) stated that "In semester length programs students are more likely to need to assimilate into the host culture and are more likely to be removed from their comfort zone, providing greater opportunity of educational experiences and cultural adaptation." Yet, beyond the program length per se, students' level of engagement may be the critical factor. Hudson and Morgan (2020) surveyed US students who participated in either a semester-long education abroad program or an international summer service-learning program in a wide variety of locations. Their findings indicated that participants' scores on a measure of engagement abroad, independent of duration, were positively related to students' growth on three GPI dimensions: Cognitive–Knowledge, Intrapersonal–Identity, and Interpersonal–Social Responsibility. Coker et al. (2018) observed that it is not surprising that longer study abroad programs appear to be superior to STSA in terms of ICC development given that for other high-impact practices, such as participation in undergraduate research, internships, and student leadership opportunities, longer programs tend to have better outcomes as well.

4.2.2 Predeparture and Reentry Interventions

There is much agreement among researchers and practitioners that predeparture training is an important component of a study abroad program (e.g., Brewer & Solberg, 2009; Deardorff, 2008; Engberg & Jourian, 2015; López & Morales, 2021; Root & Ngampornchai, 2013). In fact, Paige and Vande Berg (2012, pp. 29–30) advocated for "intentional and deliberate pedagogical approaches, activated throughout the study abroad cycle (before, during, and after), that are designed to enhance students' intercultural competence." Student sojourners often require preparation for processing their experiences abroad if they are to make gains in ICC, particularly for those on STSA programs given the diminished time for reflection during the sojourn (Brown & Cope, 2013; Engberg & Jourian, 2015; Rexeisen & Al-Khatib, 2009). In addition, predeparture interventions may be helpful in addressing students' unrealistic expectations, considering the role that expectation-experience congruence plays in sojourner satisfaction (Caligiuri et al., 2001; Martin et al., 1995; Templer et al., 2006). In a recent survey of study abroad practitioners, 64 percent expressed concern about the "disparity between student expectations and the reality of the experience" (The Forum on Education Abroad, 2017, p. 7). For example, one study found that while US students expected to encounter difficulties related to the external environment, such as language, communication, and surroundings, they did not anticipate making adjustments in terms of internal affective or cognitive factors, such as those involving stress management, identity issues, or intergroup attitudes (Goldstein & Keller, 2015). Yet most students receive little or no formal predeparture orientation (Berdan, Goodman, & Taylor, 2013), and when training does occur, it tends to focus on course content and logistics (e.g., housing, transportation, currency) rather than cultural values and expectations (Deardorff, 2008; Pilon, 2017). The rise of faculty-led STSA programs may exacerbate this problem in that the faculty involved may have greater disciplinary expertise than knowledge of, or comfort with, issues of cultural values or intergroup relations (Goode, 2007).

The study abroad literature has varied in terms of recommended predeparture training content. In an early discussion of predeparture orientation for student sojourners, Martin (1989) detailed three specific objectives: (1) providing students with a conceptual framework for understanding intercultural interactions; (2) offering students an opportunity to learn about their specific host culture; and (3) assisting students in developing strategies for adjusting to an unfamiliar culture. Thus, predeparture training was expected to be both culture-general and culture-specific (Bennett, 2008).

Several authors recommend training focused on enhancing aspects of cultural intelligence through structured experiences (e.g., Earley & Peterson, 2004; Ng et al., 2012; Şahin et al., 2014). Chang Alexander et al. (2021) developed a nine-week, on-campus cultural learning predeparture intervention focused on building students' intercultural skills guided by personalized feedback from a CQ assessment and Mor et al. (2013) suggested that it may be particularly useful to address the metacognitive skill of cultural perspective taking in intercultural training, which focuses on the ability to consider the ways in which culture may shape others' behavior (Mor et al., 2013). Root and Ngampornchai (2012, p. 526) advocated for explicitly teaching students about models of ICC. According to these authors, "If future education abroad students were aware of components of intercultural competence, it would help them place their own personal experience within the model as they engaged in intercultural experiences." Goldoni (2015, p. 4) stated that predeparture preparation should begin with an exploration of the students' own identity, based on the view that "students' integration and engagement in the host community becomes truly successful when learners understand their individual and collective identity, and how it interacts with people from other cultures and societies." Although personality traits, which are expected to be fairly stable by definition, are more challenging to alter through intercultural training than are skills and attitudes (Hannigan, 1990), Van der Zee and Van Oudenhoven (2013) advocated for training programs that target specific personality traits relevant to intercultural outcomes, such as emotional stability, flexibility, social initiative, and open-mindedness. Finally, Sit et al. (2017) conducted a systematic review to investigate the effectiveness of different types of intercultural training models for postsecondary students. Their findings indicated that intercultural training programs were more likely to result in gains in intercultural knowledge and behavioral adjustment strategies than they were to facilitate cognitive or emotional adjustment. These authors found interventions with a behavioral emphasis to be most consistently effective.

In the few studies that systematically investigated the effect of a predeparture experience on study abroad outcomes, the inclusion of predeparture training was generally supported. Chang Alexander et al. (2021) reported a statistically significant increase in three CQ domains for US students who attended a nine-week cultural learning course followed by a three-week study abroad experience in either New Zealand, Australia, or Japan, when compared with a control group of students participating in an on-campus summer scholars research program. However, it is difficult to draw conclusions about the predeparture intervention from this study since the control group differed on both the preparatory experience and the opportunity to study abroad. Paras et al. (2020) compared pre-post IDI scores for STSA participants from six institutions in Canada and the USA and reported the greatest gains for those who had participated in predeparture training, and in particular for students who attended the two programs with the most hours devoted to predeparture training (University of Guelph and St. Olaf College). Similarly, Goldstein and Smith (1999) investigated the effects of participating in a week-long predeparture program for international graduate students studying in the USA and found that those who attended the program had significantly greater CCAI scores than a matched comparison group who had not attended the predeparture training. In addition, Hanada (2019) reported that for Japanese student sojourners, having attended a predeparture program was the strongest predictor of pre-post changes in IDI scores. Finally, Kurt et al. (2013) administered a global awareness measure to participants on 23 different STSA programs at three points in time: prior to a one-credit hour preparatory course, after the predeparture course but prior to the sojourn, and after the sojourn. Although there were no significant changes following the course, these authors suggested that the predeparture course may have laid the groundwork for the subsequent gains in global awareness that occurred once abroad. Because the effect of predeparture training may not be immediately apparent, research designs comparing study abroad programs with and without a predeparture component, as opposed to those with a pre-post design, may yield more valid evidence for the impact of such interventions.

Despite the potential benefits of predeparture training for student sojourners, Chang (2017) observed that such efforts may backfire if they promote stereotyping and thus create barriers between cultural groups. Furthermore, Chao et al. (2017, p. 281) cautioned that an overemphasis on cultural differences may "inadvertently reinforce the entity cultural beliefs that each cultural group possesses immutable characteristics." A variety of research-based texts (e.g., Berdan et al., 2013; Dowell & Mirsky, 2003; Duke, 2014; Williams, 2018; Williamson, 2008), articles (e.g., Archer & Nickson, 2012; Brewer & Solberg, 2009; Brown & Cope, 2013; Goldoni, 2015; Goldstein, 2017b; Root & Ngampornchai, 2012) and other resources (e.g., La Brack, 2004; Paige et al., 2006) are available to support the development and conduct of study abroad predeparture courses.

In comparison with the limited research evaluating predeparture training for student sojourners, there has been even less attention to post–study abroad interventions. Although viewed as more logistically difficult to implement than program components prior to and during the sojourn (Pilon, 2017), there is considerable agreement on the value of reentry programming. Study abroad scholars have observed that students may emerge from their sojourn with little ability to articulate what they have learned (e.g., Pilon, 2017; Thomas & Kerstetter, 2020) or with only a superficial understanding of the host culture. For example, Root and Ngampornchai (2012) reported that study abroad participants were unable to connect surface-level cultural norms, such as those regarding food or family structure, with deeper values and cultural assumptions. In addition, they tended to frame cultural differences in terms of characteristics of the other culture rather than insights about their own cultural values. Bennett (2012) further observed that students may need assistance in transferring intercultural learning from an international to a domestic multicultural context.

4.2.3 Program Model

Study abroad program models vary significantly in terms of level of immersion and formal administrative and psychosocial support. At one end of the spectrum lies the typically more encapsulated faculty-led program as well as what has been labeled the "island" or exported campus model of study abroad (Nelson & Rapoport, 2005) in which students and faculty from a single institution live and study in a self-contained community within the host culture. At the other, more immersive end of the continuum, are direct enroll programs in which the individual is admitted to a college or university in the host country as an exchange student. Intermediate between these two models in terms of immersion are programs run by third-party providers in which independent organizations may either provide, or assist students in arranging for, housing, support services, and curricular and cocurricular content. Gozik and Oguro (2020) suggested that students from the USA have been the primary recipients of such assistance abroad, whereas students from other countries are expected to be more independent.

According to Norris and Dwyer (2005), direct enrollment is assumed by study abroad professionals to be the most effective model in achieving a range of outcomes. It is difficult to compare study abroad models given the number of other variables that may vary or covary with program model. These include characteristics of the participant (e.g., age, year in school, gender, parental status, prior intercultural experience, and predeparture intercultural and inter-group attitudes) as well as the program (e.g., duration, housing options, language use, internship opportunities; Goldstein, 2015; Norris & Dwyer, 2005; Scally, 2015). Yet the few studies that have attempted to make such comparisons have not found support for direct enrollment as the preferred model. For example, Norris and Dwyer (2005) compared outcomes for a large number of alumni from IES hybrid and facilitated direct enrollment programs. In both models the home institution or third-party provider offers academic, logistical, and cocurricular support services; however, in the hybrid programs, students have the option of taking courses from both the home institution or provider and institutions in the host country, and in facilitated direct enroll programs students take courses only at the host-country institution. Norris and Dwyer reported that although the facilitated direct enrollment respondents were more likely to have made and maintained host-country friendships, there was no statistically significant difference between students in the two models on a number of self-reported competencies including own-culture understanding, tolerance of ambiguity, intercultural interaction, interest in exploring other cultures, sophistication of world view, and subsequent travel to host country. Two other studies reported poorer outcomes for direct enroll participants. In the Georgetown Consortium study (Vande Berg et al., 2009), direct enroll participants had the lowest gains on the IDI when compared with students in less immersive models (those designed for US students alone, for international students, and hybrid) and Scally (2015) reported that students in a direct enroll program manifested lower ICC development on an author-designed pre-post survey as compared with participants in an exported campus or third-party provider program. Vande Berg et al. (2009, p. 24) suggested that these moderately immersive programs offer a balance between a challenging and a supportive environment, "Students, at one extreme, those who spent much of their free time with other US nationals were interculturally underchallenged and actually became slightly more ethnocentric while abroad. Students at the other extreme spent so much time with host country nationals that they became interculturally overwhelmed, lost ground in their IDI scores, becoming more ethnocentric."

Related to program model, group size and dynamics may also be relevant to the development of ICC. Studies indicate better ICL outcomes for those who attended programs with smaller group size (Whatley et al., 2021), experienced more comfortable dynamics (Paras et al., 2020), or reported having a peer advice network (DeJordy et al., 2020). In contrast, both Spenader and Retka (2015) and Terzuolo (2018) found no direct relation between program model and pre-post IDI scores for US students studying in a wide range of locations. Spenader and Retka suggested that pedagogical variables played a more significant role in shaping ICC gains and Terzuolo reported that participant characteristics were more critical in determining ICC outcomes. It may be useful to investigate how individual student characteristics interact with specific program models. For example, in one study, students who preferred the exported campus model scored significantly higher on ethnocentrism and lower on measures of adventurousness, language learning interest, motivational CQ, and metacognitive CQ than those who preferred a more immersive experience, such as direct enroll (Goldstein, 2015).

A relatively recent program model that has become the subject of empirical research is virtual intercultural exchange. Stemming from efforts to make student mobility more inclusive of groups underrepresented in study abroad, and spurred on by the COVID-19 pandemic and awareness of the carbon footprint associated with air travel, study abroad researchers and practitioners are increasingly exploring virtual strategies for intercultural interaction (Gwillim & Karimova, 2021; Steckley & Steckley, 2021). One of the most established of these programs is Collaborative Online International Learning (COIL; see Rubin, 2015 for a detailed history and description), in which faculty from institutions in different countries work jointly to develop an experiential and collaborative curriculum that brings their students together in a virtual platform. Similarly, a number of programs have emerged around the practice of e-volunteering (Steckley & Steckley, 2021), in which students assist an international nonprofit organization, often by conducting research to address a jointly identified area of need. Several studies using COIL and other virtual exchange curricula have reported promising results in terms of advancing students' intercultural awareness and sensitivity (e.g., Asojo et al., 2019; Chu & Torii, 2021; Coche, 2021; Gwillim & Karimova, 2021; Katre, 2020).

4.2.4 Housing

Study abroad programs vary in available housing options, which may include students living on their own, with conationals, with other international students, or with local students in apartments or university dormitories, or living with a host-country family in what is often referred to as a homestay. Although homestays tend to be the option presumed to result in the greatest intercultural learning due to the expected level of immersion (Marijuan & Sanz, 2018), findings from the few studies on this topic have been mixed, indicating little or no support for an association between homestay participation and the development of ICC (e.g., Behrnd & Porzelt, 2012; Pedersen, 2010; Spenader & Retka, 2015; Terzuolo, 2018). In fact, in the Georgetown Consortium study, students who lived with other US nationals, or with host national peers showed greater gains in ICC than those in homestays as measured by the IDI (Paige & Vande Berg, 2012).

Surprisingly, even the relationship between homestays and language learning is unclear with some studies showing slower growth in language learning for those in homestays as opposed to other housing options (Magnan & Back, 2007; Rivers, 1998; Vande Berg et al., 2009). This literature may provide some clues about the counterintuitive findings on homestays and ICC. These studies suggest that homestays may fall short in creating an immersive experience due to mismatched goals and expectations of students and host families, a situation associated with low student satisfaction with the homestay (Di Silvio et al., 2014), which may be improved through structured interactions and cultural mentoring (Marijuan & Sanz, 2018). Ogden (2007) noted a trend toward placing two or more students with a host family, which allows students to avoid moving out of their comfort zone and may decrease the frequency of intercultural contact within the homestay setting. Furthermore, students may be hesitant to engage in homestay programs. For example, one study of US undergraduates' study abroad preferences found that only 4 percent of the 252 surveyed preferred a homestay for the entire period abroad and only 9 percent were willing to participate in a homestay for a brief portion of their time abroad (Goldstein, 2019). With greater preparation and support, homestay programs may in fact facilitate the development of ICC. For example, in the Georgetown Consortium study, those homestay students who spent the most time with their host families manifested significant gains in ICC (Paige & Vande Berg, 2012). In regard to this finding, Bennet (2012, p. 8) stated, "Study abroad students in the vicinity of homestays do not necessarily have a 'homestay experience'. It is their interpreting that experience, typically through relating and communicating with the family, that generates the experience."

4.2.5 Language of Instruction

Few studies have investigated the role of language of instruction in the development of ICC. The available studies indicated that taking coursework in the host-country language appears to boost the development of ICC. In the Georgetown Consortium study, students who took classes in their host-country language had significantly higher IDI scores than those who took courses in English. Engberg and Jourian (2015), reported that students who spoke the host language inside and outside the classroom during study abroad scored higher on a measure of intercultural wonderment. Finally, Whatley et al. (2021) investigated language of instruction among potential predictors of GPI scores for US participants of STSA and reported that taking coursework in English was negatively related to nearly all subscales.

4.2.6 Internship and Service-Learning Activities

The availability of opportunities for internship and service learning abroad has expanded rapidly in recent years, along with greater attention to professional development in colleges and universities. These experiences, either integrated into study abroad programs or standalone, are assumed to promote high levels of intercultural contact and have been credited with a range of positive outcomes, including those related to career readiness, linguistic skills, and intercultural development (Gozik & Oguro, 2020; Stebleton et al., 2013). Several large studies, comparing programs with and without a service-learning or internship component support the value of these features. For example, Whatley et al. (2021) analyzed data from over 2,000 participants in STSA programs and found internships associated with significant pre-post gains in GPI scores. Spenader and Retka (2015) reported greater pre-post gains on the IDI for students on programs that involved participation in a service project alongside host nationals as compared with those that included other forms of experiential learning, such as individual research or cultural exploration projects. Varela (2017) conducted a meta-analysis of study abroad learning outcomes and found that internships and service learning were associated with significant affective gains, and nonsignificant behavioral gains, when compared with programs focused on learning in classroom settings. Varela (2017, p. 554) observed that in contrast to classroom learning, these experiences require that the student "must consciously find ways to fit into a local social unit (i.e., family, business). They must purposely reconsider their attitudes and behaviors to fulfill a social role embedded into a distinct value system."

Several study abroad scholars emphasized that in the absence of structured opportunities to process these experiences, internships and service-learning programs may have little effect on the development of ICC. Paige and Vande Berg (2012) advised that cultural mentors can play a critical role in this regard. Engberg et al. (2016) suggested that without guided reflection, internships and service learning may actually lead to unintended negative outcomes, particularly in terms of power and privilege dynamics, and thus they recommended that the design of these components prioritize building equitable partnerships between the study abroad program and member of the host community.

4.2.7 Program Location and Cultural Distance

There has long been an assumption in the study abroad world that intercultural learning is most likely to occur when students are placed in an environment significantly different from their own that takes them out of their comfort zone (Davis & Knight, 2021; Varela, 2017). Yet there has been very limited research exploring the association between cultural distance and ICC for student sojourners and the few existing studies have provided little clarity on this issue. In the literature on intercultural interaction, cultural distance refers to the degree to which the home and host culture differ. According to Triandis (1998), cultural distance can reflect differences in a wide variety of domains including language, family structure, religion, wealth and lifestyle, and values. Cultural distance has been measured using several different strategies (see, for example, Babiker et al., 1980; Muthukrishna et al., 2020) including those based on the Hofstede dimensions at the aggregate (Davis & Knight, 2021; Douglas & Jones-Rikkers, 2001; Kogut & Singh, 1988) or dimensional level (Engle & Nash, 2015), the home and host locations' level of tightness/looseness (Geeraert et al., 2019), and sojourner perceptions of cultural difference (Demes & Geeraert, 2014).

Early research on the adjustment of student sojourners (Furnham & Bochner, 1982; Ward & Kennedy, 1993) found that greater cultural distance was associated with more sociocultural adjustment difficulties. Similar findings emerged from a more recent study. Wilson et al. (2013) conducted a meta-analysis of predictors of cultural competence as assessed by the Sociocultural Adaptation Scale and reported that lower cultural distance was associated with better intercultural adjustment outcomes for various populations of sojourners. Iskhakova et al. (2021) also found that lower cultural distance was associated with greater gains in cultural intelligence (CQ) for Australian students on an STSA. Davis and Knight (2021) reported more nuanced findings based on a qualitative analysis of US semester abroad students' journals coded using GPI subscale themes. In general, they observed greater gains on the GPI knowledge dimension for students in high cultural distance placements and greater gains on the Identity dimension for those in lower cultural distance locations. Yet, in a meta-analysis of research on study abroad and intercultural learning, Varela (2017) found no support for a relation between cultural distance and cognitive, affective, or behavioral outcomes.

Based on Sanford's (1966) assertion that student sojourners learn best when there is a balance between challenge and support, Iskhakova et al. (2021) suggested that cultural distance may interact with program duration in that for students on STSA, with little time to adjust to a new environment, a smaller cultural distance may result in greater gains in ICC. In addition, the cultural distance between one's home and host culture may not accurately reflect the cultural distance between the individual and the host culture, particularly among members of minoritized groups. For example, Iskhakova et al. (2021) proposed measuring cultural distance in terms of the individual student's "nationality," rather than at the country level when considering the distance to the host country.

Finally, other aspects of the location, such as the experience of discrimination, may shape the student's perception of cultural distance and thus influence the development of ICC. Perceived discrimination has been associated with poorer intercultural adjustment outcomes for sojourners in general in a meta-analysis of correlates of cultural competence as assessed by the Sociocultural Adaptation Scale (Wilson et al., 2013). Clearly, additional research is needed to shed light on the complex relation between cultural distance and ICC. Iskhakova et al. (2021, p. 2) noted that unless factors like cultural distance are considered, "Incorrect selection decisions on participants could be made, less-efficient programmes could be designed, more distant, more expensive locations could be chosen with less desirable outcomes as a result."

4.2.8 Pedagogical Features

A final program characteristic addressed by study abroad research is pedagogical features, which include "the deliberate intercultural experiences, assignments and reflections contained within the academic coursework in a study abroad program" (Spenader & Retka, 2015, p. 22). Of these, there has been the greatest support for, and evaluation of, the often overlapping pedagogical components of cultural mentoring and guided reflection.

4.2.8.1 Cultural Mentoring

Early writing on study abroad endorsed a "sink or swim" approach in which "special treatment or coaching ... like cheating on exams, would be counter-productive and would detract from the value of the experience" (Goodwin & Nacht, 1988, p. 34). In stark contrast, and based on their analyses in the Georgetown Consortium study, Vande Berg et al. (2009, p. 25) asserted that frequent contact with a trained cultural mentor may be crucial to students' ICL while abroad. This process involves "engaging learners in ongoing discourse about their experiences, helping them better understand the intercultural nature of those encounters, and providing them with feedback relevant to their level of intercultural development" (Paige & Vande Berg, 2012, p. 53). Niehaus and Wegener (2018, p. 79) suggested that "cultural mentoring, then, stands as the vehicle by which students are able to find meaning in their study abroad experiences and transfer the competencies gained from the experience into their interactions with others." Vande Berg et al. (2009) position cultural mentoring within the context of Sanford's (1966) view that a balance between challenge and support provides the optimal learning environment. Niehaus et al. (2018) identified four types of cultural mentoring behaviors based on their survey of faculty from 72 US institutions who had recently led STSA programs. These included helping students set expectations, understand the host culture, explore themselves in relation to the host culture, and make connections across knowledge and experiences. The explicit role of cultural mentors differentiates them from programs that have support staff available for students to consult as needed. As Goertler and Schenker (2021) pointed out, this latter approach requires students' awareness that they would benefit from assistance with intercultural challenges.

The limited number of studies that have investigated the effect of cultural mentoring have supported its effectiveness in facilitating the development of ICC. In the Georgetown Consortium study (Paige & Vande Berg, 2012), students self-reported frequency of cultural mentoring predicted the greatest gains on the IDI. Engle and Engle (2004) compared IDI gains of students across six semesters at the American University Center in Provence and, although there was no control condition, they identified the extent of contact with the host culture and cultural mentoring as central to the individuals and cohorts with the greatest IDI gains. Chwialkowska (2020) surveyed over 700 international exchange students and reported that while only one in five took advantage of available mentors, those who did show greater gains in ICC. Finally, Lou and Bosley (2012) found students enrolled in the instructor-guided version of their comprehensive (predeparture, in-country, and reentry) Intentional Targeted Intervention significantly outscored their self-guided counterparts on the IDI. This latter study is significant in that the mentoring component was investigated separately from the reflection activities embedded in the content.

Several directions for future research on cultural mentoring emerge from this literature. One area that requires attention is strategies for training faculty leading STSA programs, individuals who are typically involved in the program due to their disciplinary knowledge relevant to the study abroad location. According to Pilon (2017), these faculty may lack the background to facilitate students' intercultural competence development. As Pilon (p. 143) explained, "The willingness is there; faculty need guidance on the 'how'." A second direction for future research, and perhaps a strategy to support STSA faculty, is online mentoring. Gozik and Oguro (2020) observed that in contrast to concerns about students' use of online communication while abroad that prevent a fully immersive experience, such technology has the potential to be used instead for cultural mentoring that supports greater immersion. Finally, cultural mentoring may not be a one size fits all intervention. Future investigations might explore how mentoring needs might vary by program duration (Niehaus et al., 2018) and by the personality traits, skills, and cultural awareness of the individual student (Ramirez, 2016).

4.2.8.2 Guided Reflection

Structured reflection activities have been described as a mechanism for "meaning-making" (Whatley et al., 2021) that enables students to process, solve problems, and learn from the disequilibrium that results from intercultural encounters (Engberg & Jourian, 2012). Despite widespread consensus that guided reflection plays a critical role in the ability of student sojourners to process their intercultural experiences and develop ICC (Bennett, 2008; Deardorff, 2008; Engberg, 2013; Fukuda & Nishikawa Chávez, 2021; Paige & Vande Berg, 2012; Whatley et al., 2021), there is little agreement on exactly what constitutes guided reflection. This lack of a clear definition is a significant impediment to evaluating the role of reflection activities in study abroad programming.

Perhaps the most frequently used vehicle for student reflection abroad is the personal journal. Yet Pilon (2017, p. 144) observed that without strong prompts, these tend to be used solely to record a list of daily events " . . . a log of where they went, what they saw, and what they consumed – without analyzing what they have experienced." Chang Alexander et al. (2021) provided a detailed plan for the content and timing of journal prompts based on an application of social learning theory to build cultural intelligence. They proposed that the journal document four components spread across the duration of the sojourn: (1) first impressions and expectations, (2) strategies used in applying cultural knowledge to interactions with members of the host community, (3) a taking stock of intercultural learning at the mid-point of the study abroad period, and (4) overall self-reflection and application of the experience abroad to life back home. In addition to journal entries and other writing prompts, vehicles for guided reflection have included such activities as group presentations and photographs

(Black & Bernardes, 2014), ethnography, (Lo-Philips et al., 2015), collaborative technology and social media (Lomicka & Ducate, 2021), and critical incidents (Harsch & Poehner, 2016).

Several studies of ICC outcomes attribute pre-post gains to the program's significant reflection component (e.g., Black & Bernardes, 2014; Campbell & Walta, 2015; Chiocca, 2021; Fukuda & Nishikawa Chávez, 2021). Yet few studies have systematically evaluated guided reflection. Van der Poel (2016) reported no significant difference in the IDI scores of two cohorts of Dutch students on five- to six-month sojourns, only one of which experienced an intervention designed to foster engagement and reflection. In contrast, in a study investigating the interaction between program duration and guided reflection, Pedersen (2009) compared the change in IDI scores for STSA with a guided reflection intervention to that of two, year-long programs – one with, and one without intervention as well as with a home campus control group. Among programs with intervention, there was a significantly greater change for year-long participants as compared to STSA. However, the STSA students with intervention showed greater change in IDI scores than year-long participants without intervention. Additional research is needed to elucidate the role of guided reflection in study abroad program design, including identifying the optimal form and timing of this intervention.

5 Theoretical Framework for Intercultural Competence Development through Study Abroad

Despite enthusiasm for study abroad as a means of achieving ICL, there has been very little attention to how this might occur. As support has dwindled for the *immersion assumption*, multiple scholars have called for increased attention to identifying relevant underlying processes (e.g., Fang et al., 2018; Mitchell & Paras, 2018; Reichard et al, 2015; Roy et al., 2019). Rings and Allehyani (2020, p. 20) asserted that "the precise nature of intercultural gains remains ambiguous as long as the mechanism of such development is under-researched." An understanding of this mechanism would also aid those seeking to create intercultural training materials or design optimal program content.

Several different theoretical and empirically derived approaches have clarified aspects of ICC development in student sojourners, including Deardorff's (2006) Process Model of Intercultural Competence, Mezirow's (1991) Transformative Learning Theory, Kolb's (1984) Experiential Learning Theory, and Bennett's (2004) Developmental Model of Intercultural Sensitivity (DMIS). At its core, Deardorff's Process Model of Intercultural Competence states that attitudes of respect, openness, and curiosity and discovery are foundational to the knowledge and skills needed for intercultural competence, which occurs at both an internal level (a shift in frame of reference) and an external level (effective and appropriate behavior in intercultural interactions). Mezirow's Transformative Learning Theory focuses on the process by which the learner derives meaning from – often uncomfortable – experiences in order to shift their frame of reference. And the cyclical process described by Kolb's Experiential Learning theory deals with the way that knowledge and meaning are embedded in actual experiences, such as study abroad. This latter approach involves gaining concrete experience, reflecting on that experience, engaging in abstract conceptualization of that experience, and then actively experimenting to apply what was learned. Finally, Bennett's DMIS maps the individual's movement along a continuum from ethnocentrism toward ethnorelativism as their understanding and perceptual organization of cultural differences becomes increasingly sophisticated. Additional theoretical approaches that have been applied to the development of ICC, and are discussed subsequently, include the contact hypothesis (Allport, 1954), social learning theory (Bandura, 1977), and cultural learning theory (Ward et al., 2001; Wilson et al., 2013). The framework detailed and depicted below (see Figure 1) is an attempt to integrate aspects of each of these approaches to provide a more comprehensive understanding of how study abroad may produce ICL in student sojourners. This framework does not address activities or interventions prior to or following the sojourn, which might be relevant additions in future research.

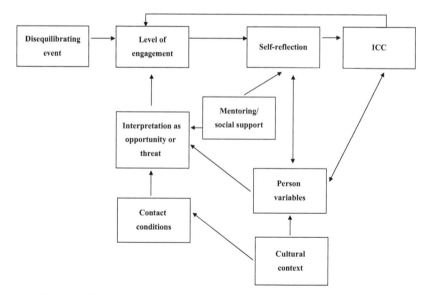

Figure 1 Theoretical framework for the development of intercultural competence via study abroad

5.1 Disequilibrating Event

Scholars of intercultural interaction have long identified disequilibrating events – experiences that challenge cultural assumptions and move the individual out of their comfort zone – as central to the development of ICC. These instances have been variously labeled as *cultural bumps* (Archer, 1991), *disorienting dilemmas* (Mezirow, 1991), *cultural trigger events* (Reichard et al., 2015), *rich points* (Agar, 1994), and *provocative moments* (Pizzolato, 2005). Certainly severely disequilibrating events are to be avoided as they may impede ICL and present threats to students' mental health. Yet even a small degree of disequilibration is no longer guaranteed in a study abroad experience. As Engle (2013, p. 111) observed:

> [H]aving based their reputations in large part on extensive student/client services, many institutions of higher learning put implicit (and sometimes explicit) pressure upon their program providers to perpetuate a recognizable version of home university expectations and comforts for their students abroad. The reluctance to challenge students with difference, at the risk of making them unhappy, has generated a culture of incompatible goals and mixed messages.

Thus, it may be difficult to achieve a balance between challenge and support in intercultural experiences, in part due to the aforementioned multiple demands on providers, but also because the appropriate level of disequilibration may vary with individual students' development over the course of the sojourn.

Despite agreement that appropriate levels of disequilibration are required to achieve gains in ICC, additional research is needed to better understand how the nature of the disequilibrating event shapes intercultural learning. For example, Mitchel and Paras (2018) suggested that the process of cognitive dissonance is key, with ICL dependent upon the specific dissonance reduction strategies enacted in response to the disequilibrating event – a hypothesis that may be complicated by cultural variation in the situations eliciting motivation for cognitive consistency (Hoshino-Browne, 2012). Another aspect of the disequilibrating event that may be worthy of investigation is the valence of the cultural comparisons involved (i.e., upward or downward). It may be that greater reexamination of ethnocentric perspectives occurs when students encounter conditions in their host culture that they view as subjectively better in some way than in their home culture.

5.2 Level of Engagement

Once faced with a disequilibrating event, students will need to determine whether and how to engage. Based on qualitative analysis of student responses to open-ended questions about their study abroad experiences, Reichard et al. (2015) identified level of engagement as the central mediator between the disequilibrating event and the development of ICC. The level of engagement determines the sojourner's access to information that forms the basis for ICL. For example, using a social learning theory framework, Chang Alexander et al. (2021) emphasized the importance of students' attention to and retention and reproduction of culturally appropriate behaviors at the point of engagement during intercultural interactions.

5.3 Interpretation of Event as Opportunity or Threat

Several factors affect whether the disequilibrating event is perceived as an opportunity or threat. Reichard et al. (2015) suggested that the availability of psychological, cognitive, and social, resources shape decisions about engagement in disequilibrating events. Mentoring may be a particularly relevant social resource in the study abroad context (Vande Berg, 2009). As will be detailed subsequently, perceptions of the disequilibrating event are also likely shaped by a wide range of person variables, including cognitive and psychological aspects, as well as by the conditions under which intercultural contact occurs.

5.4 Contact Conditions

Those seeking to understand the mechanism by which study abroad results in ICC development have also looked to Allport's (1954) contact hypothesis and subsequent elaborations, which predict improved intergroup attitudes when several conditions of contact are met, including equal status, superordinate goals, intergroup cooperation, and institutional support. For example, Engle and Crowne (2014) reported significant differences between study abroad and home campus control groups in CQ scores following participation in an STSA program that incorporated Allport's criteria. Messelink et al. (2015) suggested ICC is enhanced through institutional support manifested by integrating ICL into the curriculum. Bennett (2012), explaining why lack of growth in ICC may occur, observed that for student sojourners, the criterion of equal status contact is frequently unmet due to historical and current power imbalances and social inequalities.

5.5 Self-reflection

Reichard et al. (2015) suggested that the highest level of engagement occurs when the individual uses the new information gained in the experience to inform self-reflection. Both Transformative Learning Theory and Experiential Learning Theory consider critical self-reflection on active learning experiences as central to the ability to change one's perspective and enact learning outcomes, such as ICC development. Mezirow (1991) proposed that when faced with a dilemma, individuals reflect on the content of the problem, the process of problem-solving, or the premise of the problem itself to gain new insights. Self-reflection may also shape, and be shaped by, person variables. For example, self-efficacy may increase (van Seggelen-Damen & van Dam, 2016) and be increased by (Fritson, 2008) the process of self-reflection. Other research has indicated that resilience, central to the development of ICC, may also be enhanced by the practice of self-reflection following a stressful event (Crane et al., 2019). Finally, evidence from a review of studies on the neurocognitive bases of empathy and self-awareness suggests that self-reflection may aid individuals in understanding the thoughts and emotions of others (Dimaggio et al., 2008), and thus facilitate the development of ICC.

5.6 Mentoring and Social Support

Cultural mentors and other individuals in related roles aid ICC development by supporting students in interpreting disequilibrating events (Chwialkowska, 2020) and guiding them in making meaning of their intercultural engagement experiences through critical self-reflection (Paige & Vande Berg, 2012). Mentors from the host culture who serve as role models may be particularly impactful in the development of ICC. Varela (2017) applied social learning theory to the function of role models while abroad, noting that intercultural effectiveness is facilitated by an understanding of the cues for and value of reproducing the behavior of members of the host community.

5.7 Person Variables

As discussed earlier in this Element, several personality traits and beliefs are predictive of ICC gains during study abroad. Stress-buffering traits, such as emotional stability and flexibility, as well as social-perceptual traits, such as cultural empathy, open-mindedness, and social initiative are associated with a tendency to perceive intercultural situations as less threatening and more challenging, respectively (Van der Zee & van Oudenhoven, 2013). Additionally, person variables may shift as one develops greater ICC. Tracy-Ventura et al. (2016) reported that British students' MPQ Emotional Stability scores increased over the course of their year abroad in a French- or Spanish-speaking country. Zimmerman and Neyer (2013) found significant pre-post increases in Five-Factor Model Openness and Agreeableness as well as significant decreases in Neuroticism for German college students on both STSA and long-term study abroad programs. Cultural learning theory (Ward et al., 2001; Wilson et al.,

2013) suggests that the interculturally relevant social skills contribute to ICC and that as those skills develop, sojourners will increasingly feel comfortable engaging in the culture, which then furthers their skill set.

5.8 Cultural Context

Few articles have addressed the relation between person variables and cultural values such as individualism/collectivism vis-à-vis the development of ICC in student sojourners (Hammer, 2015). However, it seems likely that cultural values influence the set of personal characteristics the student brings to the study abroad experience. For example, Leong (2007), who reported that exchange students' social initiative was the primary predictor of intercultural adjustment, suggested that this attribute may be particularly relevant to Asian students' interactions within a Western environment. The cultural context may also affect the nature and relative importance of contact conditions. For example, a meta-analysis of 660 samples from 36 cultures indicated that contact conditions were more closely linked to intergroup relations in egalitarian as compared with hierarchical societies (Kende et al., 2018).

6 Conclusions and Future Directions

The research reviewed in this Element supports study abroad as a viable strategy for facilitating ICL among postsecondary students, with the greatest gains in cognitive, as opposed to affective or behavioral, aspects of ICC. Investigations of programs that vary widely in student population, duration, structural and pedagogical components, sending and host location, and instrumentation substantiate this conclusion. As indicated throughout this Element, with the efficacy of study abroad well established, researchers must now investigate the specific conditions most conducive to ICL.

The current review identified several reasonably consistent predictors of ICC which suggest promising avenues for best practices in study abroad program design. These include:

- Language proficiency and attitudes
- Predeparture training
- Internship and service-learning activities
- Mentoring and guided self-reflection

Interventions that increase language proficiency, language confidence, and positive attitudes about language learning may facilitate gains in ICC. This is particularly relevant to programming for US students who are far less likely than students of other nations to have studied a second language (Pew Research

Center, 2018). Predeparture training that builds intercultural skills and knowledge, as opposed to addressing course content or logistics, is also associated with ICL. Such training may also mitigate some of the disadvantages of STSA, which has the potential benefit over longer programs of greater participant inclusivity. Participation in experiential learning activities, such as community service or internships, appears to improve the likelihood of ICC gains, particularly if supported by mentoring and guided self-reflection, two key elements of study abroad programming as a whole. Additional research is needed to address inconsistencies in findings regarding other aspects of study abroad program design, such as program model, housing, and program location, as well as to explain how program components interact with each other and with participant characteristics.

There are several actions researchers might take to further efforts to identify and implement best practices for the development of ICC in student sojourners. These include:

- Identifying relevant underlying processes
- Implementing multimethod and longitudinal approaches
- Reporting detailed participant and program characteristics
- Attending to cultural bias and inclusion in conceptualizing and assessing ICC

First, researchers must strive for a clearer understanding of the mechanism underlying ICL in student sojourners, as exemplified by the framework proposed in the previous section. This would allow for the development of optimal predeparture and reentry interventions as well as in-country program design and content. Second, multimethod approaches that compensate for the potential weaknesses of self-report measures and utilize appropriate control groups are necessary to generate greater confidence in study abroad research findings. Furthermore, incorporating longitudinal designs into these approaches may result in strategies for enhancing the sustainability of ICC gains. Third, to enable replication and comparison across studies, far more detailed accounts of participant characteristics and program components should be provided in research reports. Chwialkowska (2020) observed that the lack of information on such program components as housing, academic context, and support services significantly impedes the identification of effective program design. In addition, there has been little information provided about the nature of various intercultural contact activities within programs. Wilson et al. (2013) observed that there have been few attempts to distinguish between the quality and quantity of contact with members of the host culture. Instead, program components, such as duration, language of instruction, and housing model, have – perhaps erroneously –served as a proxy for level of immersion. Finally, efforts to facilitate

ICL through study abroad cannot be successful without greater attention to cultural bias and inclusion in terms of conceptualizing and assessing ICC as well as intercultural skills and outcomes. Study abroad has evolved significantly since the "sink or swim" approach of its early years. Through the efforts of scholars and practitioners, there is much potential for further facilitating and enriching intercultural learning through study abroad.

References

Acheson, K. & Bean, S. S. (2019). Representing the intercultural development continuum as a pendulum: addressing the lived experiences of intercultural competence development and maintenance. *European Journal of Cross-Cultural Competence and Management, 5*(1), 42–61. https://doi.org/10.1504/EJCCM.2019.097826

Agar, M. (1994). *Language shock: Understanding the culture of conversation.* New York: William Morrow.

Akdere, M., Acheson, K., & Jiang, Y. (2021). An examination of the effectiveness of virtual reality technology for intercultural competence development. *International Journal of Intercultural Relations, 82,* 109–120. https://doi.org/10.1016/j.ijintrel.2021.03.009

Allport, G. W. (1954). *The nature of prejudice.* Cambridge, MA: Perseus Books.

Anderson, P. H., Lawton, L., Rexeisen, R. J., & Hubbard, A. C. (2006). Short-term study abroad and intercultural sensitivity: A pilot study. *International Journal of Intercultural Relations, 30*(4), 457–469. https://doi.org/10.1016/j.ijintrel.2005.10.004

Ang, S., Van Dyne, L., Koh, C. et al. (2007). Cultural intelligence: Its measurement and effects on cultural judgment and decision making, cultural adaptation and task performance. *Management and Organization Review, 3,* 335–371. https://doi.org/10.1111/j.1740-8784.2007.00082.x

Arasaratnam, L. A. & Doerfel, M. L. (2005). Intercultural communication competence: Identifying key components from multicultural perspectives. *International Journal of Intercultural Relations, 29,* 137–163. https://doi.org/10.1016/j.ijintrel.2004.04.001

Archer, C. M. (1991). *Living with strangers in the USA: Communicating beyond culture.* Englewood Cliffs, NJ: Prentice-Hall.

Archer, C. M. & Nickson, S. C. (2012). The role of culture bump in developing intercultural communication competency and internationalizing psychology education. *Psychology Learning and Teaching, 11,* 335–343. https://doi.org/10.2304%2Fplat.2012.11.3.335

Asojo, A., Kartoshkina, Y., Amole, D. & Jaiyeoba, B. (2019). Multicultural learning and experiences in design through the Collaborative Online International Learning (COIL) framework. *Journal of Teaching and Learning with Technology, 8,* 5–16. https://doi.org/10.14434/jotlt.v8i1.26748

Association of American Colleges and Universities (AAC&U). (2009). *Intercultural knowledge and competence VALUE rubric.* www.aacu.org/value/rubrics/inquiry-analysis

Australian Government Department of Education, Skills, and Employment (2021). *Research snapshot, March 2021.* Author. https://internationaleducation.gov.au/research/research-snapshots/Pages/default.aspx

Babiker, I. E., Cox, J. L., & Miller, P. M. C. (1980). The measurement of cultural distance and its relationship to medical consultation, symptomatology, and examination performance of overseas students at Edinburgh university. *Social Psychiatry, 15*, 109-116.

Bandura, A. (1977). *Social learning theory.* Englewood Cliffs, NJ: Prentice-Hall.

Behrnd, V. & Porzelt, S. (2012). Intercultural competence and training outcomes of students with experiences abroad. *International Journal of Intercultural Relations, 36*(2), 213–223. https://doi.org/10.1016/j.ijintrel.2011.04.005

Bennett, J. M. (2008). On becoming a global soul: A path to engagement during study abroad. In V. Savicki (Ed.), *Developing intercultural competence and transformation: Theory, research, and application in international education* (pp. 13–31). Sterling, VA: Stylus.

Bennett, M. J. (2004). Becoming interculturally competent. In J. S. Wurzel (Ed.), *Toward multiculturalism: A reader in multicultural education* (2nd ed., pp. 62–77). Newton MA:, Intercultural Resource Corporation.www.idrinstitute.org/allegati/IDRItPubblicazioni/1/FILEDocumento.pdf

Bennett, M. J. (2012). Turning cross-cultural contact into intercultural learning. *Proceedings of the Universidad 2012 8th International Congress on Higher Education, The University for Sustainable Development,* February 15, 2012, Havana, Cuba. www.idrinstitute.org/wp-content/uploads/2018/02/Turning-cross-cultural-contact.pdf

Berdan, S. N., Goodman, A. E., & Taylor, C. (2013). *A student guide to study abroad.* The Institute of International Education. New York, NY: The Institute of International Education.

Berg, T. M. V. & Schwander, L. (2019). The long-term impact of a short-term study abroad program: Perspectives on global citizenship. *Journal of Education and Learning, 8*(4), 18. https://doi.org/10.5539/jel.v8n4p18

Berry, J. W. (2003). Conceptual approaches to acculturation. In K. Chun, P. Balls-Organista, & G. Marin (Eds.), *Acculturation: Theory, method, and applications* (pp. 17–37). Washington, DC: American Psychological Association.

Berry, J. W. (2019). *Acculturation: A personal journey across cultures (Elements in Psychology and Culture).* Cambridge: Cambridge University Press.

Bhawuk, D. P. S. & Brislin, R. (1992). The measurement of intercultural sensitivity using the concepts of individualism and collectivism. *International Journal of Intercultural Relations, 16*(4), 413–436. https://doi.org/10.1016/0147-1767(92)90031-O

Black, G. L. & Bernardes, R. P. (2014). Developing global educators and intercultural competence through an international teaching practicum in Kenya. *Canadian and International Education, 43*(2), 1–15. https://doi.org/10.5206/cie-eci.v43i2.9250

Bloom, M. & Miranda, A. (2015). Intercultural sensitivity through short-term study abroad. *Language and Intercultural Communication, 15*(4), 567–580. https://doi.org/10.1080/14708477.2015.1056795

Braskamp, L. A., Braskamp, D. C. & Engberg, M. E. (2013). *Global Perspective Inventory*. Chicago, IL: Global Perspectives Institute, Inc. https://gpi.central.edu/supportDocs/manual.pdf

Bretag, T. & van der Veen, R. (2017). "Pushing the boundaries": participant motivation and self-reported benefits of short-term international study tours. *Innovations in Education and Teaching International, 54*(3), 175–183. https://doi.org/10.1080/14703297.2015.1118397

Brewer, E. & Solberg, J. (2009). Preparatory courses for students going to divergent sites: Two examples. In E. Brewer & K. Cunningham (Eds.), *Integrating study abroad into the curriculum: Theory and practice across the disciplines* (pp. 41–62). Sterling, VA: Stylus.

Brown, S. & Cope, V. (2013). Global Citizenship for the Non-Traditional Student. *Journal of Community Engagement and Scholarship, 6*(1), 28–36. https://digitalcommons.northgeorgia.edu/jces/vol6/iss1/5

Burke, M. J., Watkins, M. B., & Guzman, E. (2009). Performing in a multi-cultural context: The role of personality. *International Journal of Intercultural Relations, 33*(6), 475–485. https://doi.org/10.1016/j.ijintrel.2009.05.005

Burrow, J. D. (2019). A meta-analysis of the relationship between study abroad and intercultural competence. [Unpublished doctoral dissertation]. Toronto, Canada: University of Toronto. https://hdl.handle.net/1807/97052

Caligiuri, P., Phillips, J., Lazarova, M., Tarique, I., & Burgi, P. (2001). The theory of met expectations applied to expatriate adjustment: The role of cross-cultural training. *International Journal of Human Resource Management, 12*(3), 357–372. https://doi.org/10.1080/09585190121711

Campbell, C. J. & Walta, C. (2015). Maximizing intercultural learning in short term international placements; findings associated with orientation programs, guided reflection and immersion. *Australian Journal of Teacher Education, 40*(10), 1–15. https://doi.org/10.14221/AJTE.2015V40N10.1

Capps, J. E., Bradford, J., & Namgung, H. (2018). Promoting student engagement: The efficacy of a criminal justice short-term study abroad program. *Frontiers: The Interdisciplinary Journal of Study Abroad, 30*(3), 147–159. https://doi.org/10.36366/frontiers.v30i3.426

Carley, S. & Tudor, R. K. (2010). Assessing the impact of short-term study abroad. *Journal of Global Initiatives: Policy, Pedagogy, Perspective, 1*(2), Article 5. https://digitalcommons.kennesaw.edu/jgi/vol1/iss2/5

Chang, W.-W. (2017). Approaches for developing intercultural competence: An extended learning model with implications from cultural neuroscience. *Human Resource Development Review, 16*(2), 158–175. https://doi.org/10.1177/1534484317704292

Chang Alexander, K., Ingersoll, L. T., Calahan, C. A. et al. (2021). Evaluating an intensive program to increase cultural intelligence: A quasi-experimental design. *Frontiers: The Interdisciplinary Journal of Study Abroad, 33*(1), 106-128. https://doi.org/10.36366/frontiers.v33i1.497

Chao, M. M., Takeuchi, R., & Farh, J.-L. (2017). Enhancing cultural intelligence: The roles of implicit culture beliefs and adjustment. *Personnel Psychology, 70*(1), 257–292. https://doi.org/10.1111/peps.12142

Chen, X. & Gabrenya, W. K. (2021). In search of cross-cultural competence: A comprehensive review of five measurement instruments. *International Journal of Intercultural Relations, 82*, 37–55. https://doi.org/10.1016/j.ijintrel.2021.02.003

Chen, G.-M. & Starosta, W. J. (1996). Intercultural communication competence: A synthesis. *Communication Yearbook, 19*, 353–383.

Chen, G.-M. & Starosta, W. J. (2000). *The development and validation of the Intercultural Sensitivity Scale.* [Paper presentation]. Annual Meeting of the National Communication Association. Seattle, WA.

Chi, R. & Suthers, D. (2015). Assessing intercultural communication competence as a relational construct using social network analysis. *International Journal of Intercultural Relations, 48*, 108–119. https://doi.org/10.1016/j.ijintrel.2015.03.011

Chieffo, L. & Griffiths, L. (2004). Large-scale assessment of student attitudes after a short-term study abroad program. *Frontiers: The Interdisciplinary Journal of Study Abroad, 10*, 165–177. https://doi.org/10.36366/frontiers.v10i1.140

Chiocca, E. S. (2021). Talking with "others": Experiences and perspective transformation in a short-term study abroad program. *Frontiers: The Interdisciplinary Journal of Study Abroad, 33*(2), 35–60. https://doi.org/10.36366/frontiers.v33i2.484.

Chu, C. & Torii, Y. (2021). Communicating across cultures online: Introducing and comparing the implementation of three virtual study abroad programs. *The JACET International Convention Proceedings: The JACET 60th Commemorative International Convention*, 57–58.

Chwialkowska, A. (2020). Maximizing cross-cultural learning from exchange study abroad programs: Transformative learning theory. *Journal of Studies in International Education*, *24*(5), 535–554. https://doi.org/10.1177/10283 15320906163

Coche, R. (2021). Course internationalization through virtual exchange: Students' reflections about "seeing the world through a lens that is soccer." *Journalism & Mass Communication Educator*, *74*(4), 412–424. https://doi .org/10.1177/10776958211014074

Coker, J. S., Heiser, E., & Taylor, L. (2018). Student outcomes associated with short-term and semester study abroad programs. *Frontiers: The Interdisciplinary Journal of Study Abroad*, *30*(2), 92–105. https://doi.org/ 10.36366/frontiers.v30i2.414

Contreras, E. Jr., López-McGee, L., Wick, D., & Willis, T. (2019). Introduction: A virtual issue on diversity and inclusion in education abroad. *Frontiers: The Interdisciplinary Journal of Study Abroad*, *31*, 1–6. https://doi.org/10.36366/ frontiers.v31iVirtual.451

Cordua, F. & Netz, N. (2021). Why do women more often intend to study abroad than men? *Higher Education*. https://doi.org/10.1007/s10734-021-00731-6

Crane, M. F., Searle, B. J., Kangas, M., & Nwiran, Y. (2019). How resilience is strengthened by exposure to stressors: The systematic self-reflection model of resilience strengthening. *Anxiety, Stress & Coping: An International Journal*, *32*(1), 1–17. http://dx.doi.org/10.1080/10615806.2018.1506640

Cushner, K. (1992). The Inventory of Cross-cultural Sensitivity. In L. Kelley & A. Whatley (Eds.), *Human resource management in action: Skill building experiences* (5th ed.; pp. 176–179). St. Paul, MN: West.

Cushner, K. (2015). Development and assessment of intercultural competence. In M. Hayden, J. Levy, & J. Thompson (Eds.), *The SAGE handbook of research in international education* (2nd. ed.; pp. 200–216). Thousand Oaks, CA: Sage.

Czerwionka, L., Artamonova, T., & Barbosa, M. (2015). Intercultural knowledge development: Evidence from student interviews during short-term study abroad. *International Journal of Intercultural Relations*, *49*, 80–99. https://doi.org/10.1016/j.ijintrel.2015.06.012

Davidson, L. (2018). Measuring undergraduates' global perspective development: Examining the construct and cross-cultural validity of the Global Perspective Inventory across ethnoracial groups. [Unpublished doctoral

dissertation]. Loyola University Chicago. https://ecommons.luc.edu/luc_
diss/2950

Davies, S. C., Lewis, A. A., Anderson, A. E., & Bernstein, E. R. (2015). The
development of intercultural competency in school psychology graduate
students. *School Psychology International, 36*(4), 375–392. https://doi.org/
10.1177/0143034315592664

Davis, K. A. & Knight, D. B. (2021). Comparing students' study abroad experiences and outcomes across global contexts. *International Journal of
Intercultural Relations, 83*, 114–127. https://doi.org/10.1016/j.ijintrel
.2021.05.003

de Wit, H. & Altbach, P. G. (2021). Internationalization in higher education:
Global trends and recommendations for its future. *Policy Reviews in
Higher Education, 5*(1), 28–46. https://doi.org/10.1080/23322969.2020
.1820898

Deardorff, D. K. (2006). Identification and assessment of intercultural competence as a student outcome of internationalization. *Journal of Studies in
International Education, 10*(3), 241–266. https://doi.org/10.1177/
1028315306287002

Deardorff, D. K. (2008). Intercultural competence: A definition, model and
implications for education abroad. In V. Savicki (Ed.), *Developing intercultural competence and transformation: Theory, research, and application in international education* (pp. 32–52). Sterling, VA: Stylus.

Deardorff, D. K. (2015). Intercultural competence: Mapping the future research
agenda. *International Journal of Intercultural Relations, 48*, 3–5. https://doi
.org/10.1016/j.ijintrel.2015.03.002

Deardorff, D. K. & Jones, E. (2012). Intercultural competence: An emerging
focus in international higher education. In D. K. Deardorff, H. de Wit,
J. D. Heyl, & T. Adams (Eds.), *The SAGE handbook of international higher
education* (pp. 283–304). Thousand Oaks, CA: SAGE.

DeJordy, R., Milevoj, E., Schmidtke, J. M., & Bommer, W. H. (2020). The
success of short-term study abroad programs: a social networks perspective.
Journal of International Education in Business, 13(1), 73–86. https://doi.org/
10.1108/JIEB-08-2019-0039

Demes, K. A. & Geeraert, N. (2014). Measures matter: scales for adaptation,
cultural distance, and acculturation orientation revisited. *Journal of Cross-
Cultural Psychology, 45*(1), 91–109. https://doi.org/10.1177/00220221134
87590.

Demetry, C. & Vaz, R. (2017). Influence of an education abroad program on the
intercultural sensitivity of stem undergraduates: A mixed methods study.
Advances in Engineering Education (6), Article 1, 1–32. https://advances

.asee.org/wp-content/uploads/vol06/issue01/Papers/AEE-20-Demetry-Vaz.pdf

Dimaggio, G., Lysaker, P. H., Carcione, A., Nicolò, G., & Semerari, A. (2008). Know yourself and you shall know the other . . . to a certain extent: Multiple paths of influence of self-reflection on mindreading. *Consciousness and Cognition: An International Journal, 17*(3), 778–789. http://dx.doi.org/10.1016/j.concog.2008.02.005

Di Pietro, G. (2021). Changes in the study abroad gender gap: A European cross–country analysis. *Higher Education Quarterly.* https://doi.org/10.1111/hequ.12316

Di Silvio, F., Donovan, A., & Malone, M. E. (2014). The effect of study abroad homestay placements: Participant perspectives and oral proficiency gains. *Foreign Language Annals, 47*(1), 168–188. https://doi.org/10.1111/flan.12064

Donnelly-Smith, L. (2009). Global learning through short-term study abroad. *Association of American Colleges & Universities Peer Review, 11*(4), 1–8. www.aacu.org/peerreview/2009/fall/donnellysmith

Douglas, C. & Jones-Rikkers, C. G. (2001). Study abroad programs and American student worldmindedness: An empirical analysis. *Journal of Teaching in International Business, 13*(1), 55–66. https://doi.org/10.1300/J066v13n01_04

Dowell, M.-M. & Mirsky, K. P. (2003). *Study abroad: How to get the most out of your experience.* Upper Saddle River, NJ: Pearson.

Duke, S. T. (2014). *Preparing to study abroad: Learning to cross cultures.* Sterling, VA: Stylus.

Dukes, R., Lockwood, E., Oliver, H., Pezalla, C., & Wilker, C. (1994). A longitudinal study of a semester at sea voyage. *Annals of Tourism Research,* 21(3), 489–498. https://doi.org/10.1016/0160-7383(94)90116-3

Dwyer, M. M. (2004). More is better: The impact of study abroad program duration. *Frontiers: The Interdisciplinary Journal of Study Abroad, 10,* 151–163. www.frontiersjournal.com/index.htm

Earley, P. C. & Peterson, R. S. (2004). The elusive cultural chameleon: Cultural intelligence as a new approach to intercultural training for the global manager. *Academy of Management Learning and Education, 3*(1), 100–115. https://psycnet.apa.org/doi/10.5465/AMLE.2004.12436826

Engberg, M. E. (2013). The influence of study away experiences on global perspective-taking. *Journal of College Student Development, 54*(5), 466–480. https://doi.org/10.1353/csd.2013.0073

Engberg, M. E. & Jourian, T. J. (2015). Intercultural wonderment and study abroad. *Frontiers: The Interdisciplinary Journal of Study Abroad, 25,* 1–19. https://doi.org/10.36366/frontiers.v25i1.341

Engberg, M. E., Jourian, T. J., & Davidson, L. M. (2016). The mediating role of intercultural wonderment: connecting programmatic components to global outcomes in study abroad. *Higher Education, 71*, 21–37. https://doi.org/10.1007/S10734-015-9886-6

Earley, P. C. & Peterson, R. S. (2004). The elusive cultural chameleon: Cultural intelligence as a new approach to intercultural training for the global manager. *Academy of Management Learning & Education, 3*(1), 100–115. https://doi.org/10.5465/AMLE.2004.12436826

Engle, L. (2013). The rewards of qualitative assessment appropriate to study abroad. *Frontiers: The Interdisciplinary Journal of Study Abroad, 22*(1), 111–126. https://doi.org/10.36366/frontiers.v22i1.321

Engle, L. & Engle, J. (2003). Study abroad levels: Toward a classification of program types. *Frontiers: The Interdisciplinary Journal of Study Abroad, 9*, 1–20. https://doi.org/10.36366/frontiers.v9i1.113

Engle, L. & Engle, J. (2012). Beyond immersion: The American University Center of Provence experiment in holistic intervention. In M. Vande Berg, R. M. Paige, & K. H. Lou (Eds.), *Student learning abroad: What our students are learning, what they're not, and what we can do about it* (pp.284–307). Sterling, Virginia: Stylus.

Engle, R. L. & Crowne, K. A. (2014). The impact of international experience on cultural intelligence: an application of contact theory in a structured short-term programme. *Human Resource Development International, 17*(1), 30–46. https://doi.org/10.1080/13678868.2013.856206

Engle, R. L. & Nash, B. (2015). Does it matter if researchers use individual dimension constructs or only aggregated constructs of cultural distance and cultural intelligence? *Journal of International Business Research, 14*(2), 47–65. http://refhub.elsevier.com/S2212-571X(16)30180-9/sbref26

Erasmus (2021). *Erasmus + factsheet.* Author. Luxembourg: Publications Office of the European Union https://eurireland.ie/assets/uploads/2021/03/Factsheet.pdf

Fang, F., Schei, V., & Selart, M. (2018). Hype or hope? A new look at the research on cultural intelligence. *International Journal of Intercultural Relations, 66*, 148–171. https://doi.org/10.1016/j.ijintrel.2018.04.002

Fantini, A. & Tirmizi, A. (2006). Exploring and assessing intercultural competence. *World Learning Publications.* Paper 1. http://digitalcollections.sit.edu/worldlearning_publications/1

Fritson, K. K. (2008). Impact of journaling on students' self-efficacy and locus of control. *Insight: A Journal of Scholarly Teaching, 3*, 75–83. http://dx.doi.org/10.46504/03200809fr

Fukuda, M. & Nishikawa Chávez, K. (2021). Summer study abroad in Japan: Maximizing intercultural competency development through self-guided cultural exploration and reflection tasks. *Foreign Language Annals.* Advance online publication. https://doi.org/10.1111/flan.12556

Furnham, A. & Bochner, S. (1982). Social difficulty in a foreign culture: An empirical analysis of culture shock. In S. Bochner (Ed.), *Cultures in contact* (pp. 161–198). New York, NY: Pergamon. https://doi.org/10.1016/B978-0-08-025805-8.50016-0

Gaia, A. C. (2015). Short-term faculty-led study abroad programs enhance cultural exchange and self-awareness. *The International Education Journal: Comparative Perspectives, 14*(1), 21–31.

Geeraert, N., Li, R., Ward, C., Gelfand, M., & Demes, K. A. (2019). A tight spot: How personality moderates the impact of social norms on sojourner adaptation. *Psychological Science, 30*(3), 333–342. https://doi.org/10.1177/0956797618815488

Giovanangeli, A. & Oguro, S. (2016). Cultural Responsiveness: A framework for re-thinking students' interculturality through study abroad. *Intercultural Education, 27*(1), 70–84. https://doi.org/10.1080/14675986.2016.1144328

Goertler, S. & Schenker, T. (2021). *From study abroad to education abroad: Language proficiency, intercultural competence, and diversity.* New York, NY: Routledge.

Goldoni, F. (2015). Preparing students for studying abroad. *Journal of the Scholarship of Teaching and Learning, 15*(4), 1–20. https://doi.org/10.14434/josotl.v15i4.13640

Goldstein, D. L. & Smith, D. H. (1999). The analysis of the effects of experiential training on sojourners' cross cultural adaptability. *International Journal of Intercultural Relations, 23*(1), 157–173. https://doi.org/10.1016/S0147-1767(98)00030-3

Goldstein, S. B. (2015). Predictors of preference for the exported campus model of study abroad. *Frontiers: The Interdisciplinary Journal of Study Abroad, 26*, 1–16. https://doi.org/10.36366/frontiers.v26i1.351

Goldstein, S. B. (2017a). Stereotype threat in U.S. students abroad: Negotiating American identity in the age of Trump. *Frontiers: The Interdisciplinary Journal of Study Abroad, 29*(2), 94–108. https://doi.org/10.36366/frontiers.v29i2.395

Goldstein, S. B. (2017b). Teaching a psychology-based study abroad pre-departure course. *Psychology Learning and Teaching, 16*(3), 404–424. https://doi.org/10.1177%2F1475725717718059

Goldstein, S. B. (2019). Support for a multidimensional model of study abroad immersion preference. *Frontiers: The Interdisciplinary Journal of Study Abroad, 31*(1), 1–21. https://doi.org/10.36366/frontiers.v31i1.440

Goldstein, S. B. (2022). A systematic review of short-term study abroad research methodology and intercultural competence outcomes. *International Journal of Intercultural Relations, 87,* 26–36.

Goldstein, S. B. & Keller, S. R. (2015). U. S. college students' lay theories of culture shock. *International Journal of Intercultural Relations, 47,* 187–194. https://doi.org/10.1016/j.ijintrel.2015.05.010

Goldstein, S. B. & Kim, R. I. (2006). Predictors of U. S. college students' participation in study abroad programs: A longitudinal study. *International Journal of Intercultural Relations, 30,* 507–521. https://doi.org/10.1016/j.ijintrel.2005.10.001

Gondra, A. & Czerwionka, L. (2018). Intercultural knowledge development during short-term study abroad in the Basque Country: A cultural and linguistic minority context. *Frontiers: The Interdisciplinary Journal of Study Abroad, 30,* 119–146. https://doi.org/10.36366/frontiers.v30i3.427

Goode, M. L. (2007). The role of faculty study abroad directors: A case study. *Frontiers: The Interdisciplinary Journal of Study Abroad, 15,* 149–172. https://doi.org/10.36366/frontiers.v15i1.224

Goodwin, C. D. & Nacht, M. (1988). *Abroad and beyond: Patterns in American overseas education.* Cambridge: Cambridge University Press.

Gower, S., Duggan, R., Dantas, J. A. R., & Boldy, D. (2019). One year on: Cultural competence of Australian nursing students following international service-learning. *The Journal of Nursing Education, 58*(1), 17–26. https://doi.org/10.3928/01484834-20190103-04

Gozik, N. & Oguro, S. (2020). Program components: (Re)considering the role of individual areas of programming in education abroad. In A. C. Ogden, B. Streitwieser, & C. Van Mol (Eds.). *Education abroad: Bridging scholarship and practice* (pp. 59–72). London: Routledge.

Granel, N. et al. (2021). Student's satisfaction and intercultural competence development from a short study abroad programs: A multiple cross-sectional study. *Nurse Education in Practice, 50,* 1–6. https://doi.org/10.1016/j.nepr.2020.102926

Griffith, R. L., Wolfeld, L., Armon, B. K., Rios, J., & Liu, O. L. (2016). *Assessing intercultural competence in higher education: Existing research and future directions* (ETS Research Report No. RR-16-25). Educational Testing Service. https://doi.org/10.1002/ets2.12112

Gullekson, N. L., Tucker, M. L., Coombs, G., & Wright, S. B. (2011). Examining intercultural growth for business students in short-term study abroad programs: Too good to be true? *Journal of Teaching in International Business, 22*(2), 91–106. https://doi.org/10.1080/08975930.2011.615672

Gwillim, T. D. & Karimova, I. I. (2021). Virtual exchanges: Fake mobility or unique experiences. *Universal Journal of Educational Research, 9*(2), 373–379. http://dx.doi.org/10.13189/ujer.2021.090213

Haas, B. W. (2018). The impact of study abroad on improved cultural awareness: A quantitative review. *Intercultural Education, 29*(5–6), 571–588. https://doi.org/10.1080/14675986.2018.1495319

Hammer, M. R. (2011). Additional cross-cultural validity testing of the intercultural development inventory. *International Journal of Intercultural Relations, 35*(4), 474–487. https://psycnet.apa.org/doi/10.1016/j.ijintrel.2011.02.014

Hammer, M. R. (2015). The Developmental paradigm for intercultural competence research. *International Journal of Intercultural Relations, 48*, 12–13. https://doi.org/10.1016/j.ijintrel.2015.03.004

Hammer, M. & Bennett, M. (2002) *The Intercultural Development Inventory: Manual.* Portland, OR: Intercultural Communication Institute.

Hanada, S. (2019). A quantitative assessment of Japanese students' intercultural competence developed through study abroad programs. *Journal of International Students, 9*(4), 1015–1037. https://doi.org/10.32674/jis.v9i4.391

Hannigan, T. F. (1990). Traits, attitudes, and skills that are related to intercultural effectiveness and their implications for cross-cultural training: A review of the literature. *International Journal of Intercultural Relations, 14*(1), 89–111. https://doi.org/10.1016/0147-1767(90)90049-3

Harris, V. W., Kumaran, M., Harris, H. J., Moen, D., & Visconti, B. (2019). Assessing multicultural competence (knowledge and awareness) in study abroad experiences. *Compare: A Journal of Comparative and International Education, 49*(3), 430–452. https://doi.org/10.1080/03057925.2017.1421901

Harrison, N. (2012). Investigating the impact of personality and early life experiences on intercultural interaction in internationalized universities. *International Journal of Intercultural Relations, 36*(2), 224–237. https://doi.org/10.1016/j.ijintrel.2011.03.007

Harsch, C. & Poehner, M. E. (2016). Enhancing student experiences abroad: the potential of dynamic assessment to develop student interculturality. *Language and Intercultural Communication, 16*(3), 470–490. https://doi.org/10.1080/14708477.2016.1168043

Heinzmann, S., Künzle, R., Schallhart, N., & Müller, M. (2015). The effect of study abroad on intercultural competence: Results from a longitudinal quasi-experimental study. *Frontiers: The Interdisciplinary Journal of Study Abroad*, *26*(1), 187–208. https://doi.org/10.36366/frontiers.v26i1.366

Hett, E. J. (1993). *The development of an instrument to measure global-mindedness* [Unpublished doctoral dissertation]. University of San Diego. https://digital.sandiego.edu/cgi/viewcontent.cgi?article=1589&context=dissertations

Hofer, B. K., Thebodo, S. W., Meredith, K., Kaslow, Z., & Saunders, A. (2016). The long arm of the digital tether: Communication with home during study abroad. *Frontiers: The Interdisciplinary Journal of Study Abroad*, *28*, 24–41. https://doi.org/10.36366/frontiers.v28i1.378

Hoshino-Browne, E. (2012). Cultural variations in motivation for cognitive consistency: Iinfluences of self-systems on cognitive dissonance. *Social and Personality Psychology Compass 6*(2), 126–141. https://doi.org/10.1111/j.1751-9004.2011.00419.x

Hudson, T. D. & Morgan, R. T. (2020). Examining relationships between education abroad program design and college students' global learning. *Frontiers: The Interdisciplinary Journal of Study Abroad*, 31(2),1–31. https://doi.org/10.36366/frontiers.v31i2.452

Ingraham, E. C. & Peterson, D. L. (2004). Assessing the impact of study abroad on student learning at Michigan State University. *Frontiers: The Interdisciplinary Journal of Study Abroad*, *10*(1), 83–100. https://doi.org/10.36366/frontiers.v10i1.134

Institute of International Education (2020). Detailed duration of U.S. Study Abroad, 2005/06 – 2018/19. Open doors report on international educational exchange. https://opendoorsdata.org/

International Education Association of Australia (2016). *Outcomes of learning abroad programs*. Author. Melbourne, Australia: International Education Association of Australia. www.ieaa.org.au/documents

Iqbal, Z. (2020). Eastern promises fulfilled: The differential impact of marketing-focused short-term study abroad programs in India and Japan. *Frontiers: The Interdisciplinary Journal of Study Abroad*, *31*(2), 158–179. https://doi.org/10.36366/frontiers.v31i2.460

Iskhakova, M., Bradly, A., Whiting, B., & Lu, V. N. (2021). Cultural intelligence development during short-term study abroad programmes: The role of cultural distance and prior international experience. *Studies in Higher Education*, 1–18. https://doi.org/10.1080/03075079.2021.1957811

Jackson, J. (2015). Becoming interculturally competent: Theory to practice in international education. *International Journal of Intercultural Relations*, *48*, 91–107. https://doi.org/10.1016/j.ijintrel.2015.03.012

Johnson, L. E. & Battalio, R. (2008). Expanding the boundaries of special education preservice teachers: The impact of a six-week special education study abroad program. *International Journal of Special Education*, 23(3), 90–100.

Kartoshkina, Y., Chieffo, L., & Kang, T. (2013). Using an internally-developed tool to assess intercultural competence in short-term study abroad Programs. *International Research and Review*, 3(1), 23–39. www.phibetadelta.org/pdf/ IRR%20FALL%202013%20-%20V3N1.pdf

Kato, M. & Suzuki, K. (2019). Effective or self-selective: Random assignment demonstrates short-term study abroad effectively encourages further study abroad. *Journal of Studies in International Education*, 23(4), 411–428. https://doi.org/10.1177/1028315318803713

Katre, A. (2020). Creative economy teaching and learning – A collaborative online international learning case. *International Education Studies*, 13(7), 145–155. http://dx.doi.org/10.5539/ies.v13n7p145

Kealey, D. J. (2015). Some strengths and weaknesses of 25 years of research on intercultural communication competence: Personal reflections. *International Journal of Intercultural Relations*, 48, 14–16. https://doi.org/10.1016/j.ijintrel .2015.03.00

Kehl, K. & Morris, J. (2008). Differences in global-mindedness between short-term and semester-long study abroad participants at selected private universities. *Frontiers: The Interdisciplinary Journal of Study Abroad*, 15, 67–79. https://doi.org/10.36366/frontiers.v15i1.217

Kelley, C. & Meyers, J. (1995). *CCAI: Cross-cultural adaptability inventory.* Bloomington, MN: NCS Pearson.

Kende, J., Phalet, K., Van den Noortgate, W., Kara, A., & Fischer, R. (2018). Equality revisited: A cultural meta-analysis of intergroup contact and prejudice. *Social Psychological and Personality Science*, 9(8), 887–895. https://doi.org/10.1177%2F1948550617728993

Kilgo, C., Ezell Sheets, J., & Pascarella, E. (2015). The link between high-impact practices and student learning: Some longitudinal evidence. *Higher Education*, 69, 509–525. http://dx.doi.org/10.1007/s10734-014-9788-z

Kim, H. S. & Lawrence, J. H. (2021). Who studies abroad? Understanding the impact of intent on participation. *Research in Higher Education*, 62, 1039–1085. https://doi.org/10.1007/s11162-021-09629-9

Kim, R. I. & Goldstein, S. B. (2005). Intercultural attitudes predict favorable study abroad expectations of American college students. *Journal of Studies in International Education*, 9, 265–278. https://doi.org/10.1177/102831530 5277684

King, P. M. & Baxter Magolda, M. B. (2005). A developmental model of intercultural maturity. *Journal of College Student Development, 46*(6), 571–592. https://doi.org/10.1353/csd.2005.0060

Kitsantas, A. (2004). Studying abroad: The role of college students' goals on the development of cross-cultural skills and global understanding. *College Student Journal, 38*(3), 441–452.

Koester, J. & Lustig, M. W. (2015). Intercultural communication competence: Theory, measurement, and application. *International Journal of Intercultural Relations, 48*, 20–21. https://doi.org/10.1016/j.ijintrel.2015.03.006

Kogut, B. & Singh, H. (1988). The effect of national culture on the choice of entry mode. *Journal of International Business Studies, 19*, 411–432.

Kolb, D. A. (1984). *Experiential learning: Experience as the source of learning and development* (Vol. 1). Englewood Cliffs, NJ: Prentice-Hall.

Kozai Group. (2009). *The intercultural effectiveness scale.* Chesterfield, MO: Kozai Group. www.kozaigroup.com/wp-content/uploads/2015/09/IES_Guide.pdf

Krishnan, L. A., Diatta-Holgate, H., & Calahan, C. A. (2021). Intercultural competence gains from study abroad in India. *Teaching and Learning in Communication Sciences & Disorders, 5* (4), Article 6. https://ir.library.illinoisstate.edu/tlcsd/vol5/iss2/6

Kuh, G. D. (2008). *High-impact educational practices: What they are, who has access to them, and why they matter.* Washington, DC: Association of American Colleges and Universities.

Kurt, M., Olitsky, N., & Geis, P. (2013). Assessing global awareness over short-term study abroad sequence: A factor analysis. *Frontiers: The Interdisciplinary Journal of Study Abroad, 23*(1), 22–41. https://doi.org/10.36366/frontiers.v23i1.327

La Brack, B. (2004). What's up with culture?: On-line cultural training resource for study abroad. Stockton, CA: University of the Pacific. http://www2.pacific.edu/sis/culture

Lee, E. J., Lee, L., & Jang, J. (2010). Internet for the internationals: Effects of internet use motivations on international students' college adjustment. *Cyberpsychology, Behavior & Social Networking, 14*(7/8), 433–437. https://doi.org/10.1089/cyber.2010.0406

Leong, C. (2007). Predictive validity of the Multicultural Personality Questionnaire: A longitudinal study on the socio-psychological adaptation of Asian undergraduates who took part in a study-abroad program. *International Journal of Intercultural Relations, 31*, 545–559. https://doi.org/10.1016/j.ijintrel.2007.01.004

Lewis, T. L. & Niesenbaum, R. A. (2005). Extending the stay: Using community-based research and service learning to enhance short-term study abroad. *Journal of Studies in International Education, 9*(3), 251–264. https://doi.org/10.1177/1028315305277682

Li, M., Olson, J. E., & Frieze, I. H. (2013). Students' study abroad plans: The influence of motivational and personality factors. *Frontiers: The Interdisciplinary Journal of Study Abroad, 23*(1), 73–89. https://doi.org/10.36366/frontiers.v23i1.330

Lieberman, D. A. & Gamst, G. (2015). Intercultural communication competence revisited: Linking the intercultural and multicultural fields. *International Journal of Intercultural Relations, 48*, 17–19. https://doi.org/10.1016/j.ijintrel.2015.03.007

Lomicka, L. & Ducate, L. (2021). Using technology, reflection, and noticing to promote intercultural learning during short-term study abroad. *Computer Assisted Language Learning, 34*(1–2), 35–65. https://doi.org/10.1080/09588221.2019.1640746

Lo-Philip, S. W. Y. et al. (2015). Transforming educational practices: Cultural learning for short-term sojourners. *International Journal of Intercultural Relations, 49*, 223–234. https://doi.org/10.1016/j.ijintrel.2015.10.006

López, M. M. & Morales, P. R. L. (2021). From global south to global north: Lessons from a short-term study abroad program for Chilean teacher candidates in English pedagogy. *Journal of Research in Childhood Education, 35*(2), 248–267. https://doi.org/10.1080/02568543.2021.1880997

Lou, K. H. & Bosley, G. W. (2012). Facilitating intercultural learning abroad. In M. Vande Berg, M. Paige, & K. H. Lou (Eds.), *Students learning abroad: What our students are learning, what they're not, and what we can do about it* (pp. 355–359). Sterlng, VA: Stylus.

Lu, C., Reddick, R., Dean, D., & Pecero, V. (2015). Coloring up study abroad: Exploring Black students' decision to study in China. *Journal of Student Affairs Research and Practice, 52*(4), 440–451. https://doi.org/10.1080/19496591.2015.1050032

Lumkes, J. H., Hallett, S., & Vallade, L. (2012). Hearing versus experiencing: The impact of a short-term study abroad experience in China on students' perceptions regarding globalization and cultural awareness. *International Journal of Intercultural Relations, 36*(1), 151–159. https://doi.org/10.1016/j.ijintrel.2011.12.004

Magnan, S. S. & Back, M. (2007). Social interaction and linguistic gain during study abroad. *Foreign Language Annals, 40*(1), 43–61. https://doi.org/10.1111/j.1944-9720.2007.tb02853.x

Mahon, J. A. & Cushner, K. (2014). Revising and updating the inventory of cross-cultural sensitivity. *Intercultural Education, 25*(6), 484–496. https://doi.org/10.1080/14675986.2014.990232

Makara, M. & Canon, K. (2020). More than a vacation? Assessing the impact of a short-term study abroad program to the Middle East. *Journal of Political Science Education, 16*(3), 314–334. https://doi.org/10.1080/15512169.2019.1599292

Malewski, E., Sharma, S., & Phillion, J. (2012). How international field experiences promote cross-cultural awareness in preservice teachers through experiential learning: Findings from a six-year collective case study. *Teachers College Record, 114*, 1–44.

Mapp, S. C., McFarland, P., & Newell, E. A. (2007). The effect of a short-term study abroad class on students' cross-cultural awareness. *The Journal of Baccalaureate Social Work, 13*(1), 39–51.

Marijuan, S. & Sanz, C. (2018). Expanding boundaries: Current and new directions in study abroad research and practice. *Foreign Language Annals, 51*(1), 185–204. https://doi.org/10.1111/flan.12323

Martin, J. N. (1989). Predeparture orientation: Preparing college sojourners for intercultural interaction. *Communication Education, 38*, 249–258. https://doi.org/10.1080/03634528909378761

Martin, J. N. (2015). Revisiting intercultural communication competence: Where to go from here. *International Journal of Intercultural Relations, 48*, 6–8. https://doi.org/10.1016/j.ijintrel.2015.03.008

Martin, J. N., Bradford, L., & Rohrlich, B. (1995). Comparing predeparture expectations and post-sojourn reports: A longitudinal study of U.S. students abroad. *International Journal of Intercultural Relations, 19*, 87–110.

Masgoret, A.-M. & Ward, C. (2006). Culture learning approaches to acculturation. In D. L. Sam, & J. W. Berry (Eds.), *The Cambridge handbook of acculturation psychology* (pp. 58–77). Cambridge: Cambridge University Press.

Matsumoto, D. & Hwang, H. C. (2013). Assessing cross-cultural competence. *Journal of Cross-Cultural Psychology, 44*(6), 849–873. https://doi.org/10.1177/0022022113492891

McKeown, J. S. (2009). *The first time effect: The impact of study abroad on college student intellectual development.* Albany, NY: State University of New York Press.

Medina-Lopez-Portillo, A. (2004). Intercultural learning assessment: The link between program duration and the development of intercultural sensitivity. *Frontiers: The Interdisciplinary Journal of Study Abroad, 10*, 179–199. https://doi.org/10.36366/frontiers.v10i1.141

Messelink, H. E. & ten Thije, J. (2012). Unity in super-diversity: European capacity and intercultural inquisitiveness of the Erasmus generation 2.0. *Dutch Journal for Applied Linguistics*, *1*, 81–101. http://dx.doi.org/10.1075/dujal.1.1.07mes

Messelink, H. E., van Maele, J., & Spencer-Oatey, H. (2015). Intercultural competencies: What students in study and placement mobility should be learning. *Intercultural* Education, *26*(1), 62–72. https://doi.org/10.1080/14675986.2015.993555

Mezirow, J. (1991). *Transformative dimensions of adult learning*. San Francisco: Jossey-Bass.

Mitchell, L. & Paras, A. (2018). When difference creates dissonance: understanding the "engine" of intercultural learning in study abroad. *Intercultural Education*, *29*(3), 321–339. https://doi.org/10.1080/14675986.2018.1436361

Miville, M. L. et al. (1999). Appreciating similarities and valuing differences: The Miville-Guzman Universality-Diversity Scale. *Journal of Counseling Psychology*, *46*(3), 291–307. https://doi.org/10.1037/0022-0167.46.3.291

Mo l, S., Van Oudenhoven, J. P., & Van der Zee, K. I. (2001). Validation of the M.P.Q. amongst an internationally oriented student population in Taiwan. In F. Salili, & R. Hoosain (Eds.), *Research in multicultural education and international perspectives* (pp. 167–186). Greenwich, CT: Information Age.

Mor, S., Morris, M., & Joh, J. (2013). Identifying and training adaptive cross-cultural management skills: The crucial role of cultural metacognition. *Academy of Management Learning & Education*, *12*(3), 453–475. https://doi.org/10.5465/amle.2012.0202

Mule, L. W., Audley, S., & Aloisio, K. (2018). Short-term, faculty-led study abroad and global citizenship identification: Insights from a global engagement program. *Frontiers: The Interdisciplinary Journal of Study Abroad*, *30*(3), 20–37. https://frontiersjournal.org/index.php/Frontiers/article/view/425

Muthukrishna, M. et al. (2020). Beyond western, educated, industrial, rich, and democratic (WEIRD) psychology: Measuring and mapping scales of cultural and psychological distance. *Psychological science*, *31*(6), 678–701. https://doi.org/10.1177/0956797620916782

Nelson, L. R. & Rapoport, A. (2005). Russian civic education and social studies education at Purdue University. *International Journal of Social Education*, *20*(2), 99–114.

Nerlich, S. (2016). Counting outward mobility: The data sources and their constraints. In D. M. Velliaris & D. Coleman-George (Eds.), *Handbook of research on study abroad programs and outbound mobility* (pp. 40–65). Hershey, PA: Information Science Reference.

Ng, K. Y., Van Dyne, L., & Ang, S. (2012). Cultural intelligence: A review, reflections, and recommendations for future research. In A. M. Ryan, F. T. L. Leong, & F. L. Oswald (Eds.), *Conducting multinational research: Applying organizational psychology in the workplace* (pp. 29–58). Washington, DC: American Psychological Association. https://doi.org/10.1037/13743-002

Nguyen, A. (2017). Intercultural competence in short-term study abroad. *Frontiers: The Interdisciplinary Journal of Study Abroad, 29*(2), 109–127. https://frontiersjournal.org/index.php/Frontiers/article/view/396

Nguyen, A.-M. D. (2013). Acculturation. In K. Keith (Ed.), *Encyclopedia of cross-cultural psychology* (pp. 7–12). London: Wiley-Blackwell.

Nguyen, A.-M. D., Jefferies, J., & Rojas, B. (2018). Short term, big impact? Changes in self-efficacy and cultural intelligence, and the adjustment of multicultural and monocultural students abroad. *International Journal of Intercultural Relations, 66*, 119–129. https://doi.org/10.1016/j.ijintrel.2018.08.001

Niehaus, E. & Wegener, A. (2018). What are we teaching abroad? Faculty goals for short-term study abroad courses. *Innovative Higher Education, 44*(2), 103–117. https://doi.org/10.1007/s10755-018-9450-2

Norris, E. M. & Dwyer, M. M. (2005). Testing assumptions: The impact of two study abroad program models. *Frontiers: The Interdisciplinary Journal of Study Abroad, 11*, 121–142. https://doi.org/10.36366/frontiers.v11i1.154

Nowlan, A. & Wang, R. (2018). Study abroad self-selection amongst first-year Japanese university students. *Journal of International and Comparative Education, 7*(2), 65–81.

Ogden, A. (2007). The view from the veranda: Understanding today's colonial student. *Frontiers: The Interdisciplinary Journal of Study Abroad, 15*(1), 35–56. https://doi.org/10.36366/frontiers.v15i1.215

Ogden, A. C. (2015). *Toward a research agenda for U.S. education abroad.* Durham, NC: Association of International Education Administrators. www.aieaworld.org/assets/docs/research agenda/ogden 2015.pdf

Olson, C. L. & Kroeger, K. R. (2001). Global Competency and intercultural sensitivity, *Journal of Studies in International Education, 5*, 116–137. https://doi.org/10.1177/102831530152003

Opengart, R. (2018). Short-term study abroad and the development of intercultural maturity. *Journal of International Education in Business, 11*(2), 241–255. https://doi.org/10.1108/JIEB-02-2017-0009

Ota, H. (2018). Internationalization of higher education: Global trends and Japan's challenges. *Educational Studies in Japan: International Yearbook, 12*, 91–105. https://doi.org/10.7571/ESJKYOIKU.12.91

Ott, D. L. & Iskhakova, M. (2019). The meaning of international experience for the development of cultural intelligence: A review and critique. *Critical Perspectives on International Business, 15*(4), 390–407. http://dx.doi.org/10.1108/cpoib-05-2019-0036

Paige, R. M., Cohen, A. D., Kappler, B., Chi, J. C., & Lassegard, J. P. (2006). *Maximizing study abroad: A student's guide to strategies for language and culture learning and use* (2nd ed.). Minneapolis, MN: Center for Advanced Research on Language Acquisition, University of Minnesota.

Paige, R. M., Fry, G., Stallman, E., Josić, J., & Jon, J.-E. (2009). Study abroad for global engagement: The long-term impact of mobility experiences. *Intercultural Education, 20*, S29–S44. https://doi.org/10.1080/1467598090 3370847

Paige, M. & Vande Berg, M. (2012). Why students are not learning abroad. In M. Vande Berg, M. Paige, & K. H. Lou (Eds.), *Students learning abroad: What our students are learning, what they're not, and what we can do about it* (pp. 29–58). Sterling, VA: Stylus.

Paras, A. et al. (2020). Understanding how program factors influence intercultural learning in study abroad: The benefits of mixed-method analysis. *Frontiers: The Interdisciplinary Journal of Study Abroad, 31*(1), 22–45. https://doi.org/10.36366/frontiers.v31i1.441

Pedersen P. J. (2009). Teaching towards and ethnorelative worldview through psychology study abroad. *Intercultural Education, 20*(1–2), S73–86. https://doi.org/10.1080/14675980903370896

Pedersen, P. J. (2010). Assessing intercultural effectiveness outcomes in a year-long study abroad program. *International Journal of Intercultural Relations, 34*(1), 70–80. https://doi.org/10.1016/j.ijintrel.2009.09.003

Peifer, J. S., Meyer-Lee, E., & Taasoobshirazi, G. (2021). Developmental pathways to intercultural competence in college students. *Journal of Studies in International Education*, 102831532110527. https://doi.org/10.1177/10283153211052778

Peng, R.-Z. & Wu, W.-P. (2016). Measuring intercultural contact and its effects on intercultural competence: A structural equation modeling approach. *International Journal of Intercultural Relations, 53*, 16–27. https://doi.org/10.1016/j.ijintrel.2016.05.003

Peng, R.-Z., Wu, W.-P.,& Fan, W. -W. (2015). A comprehensive evaluation of Chinese college students' intercultural competence. *International Journal of Intercultural Relations, 47*, 143–157. https://doi.org/10.1016/j.ijintrel.2015 .04.003

Pew Research Center (August 6, 2018). Most European students are learning a foreign language in school while Americans lag. Author. Washington, DC:

Pew Research Center. www.pewresearch.org/fact-tank/2018/08/06/most-european-students-are-learning-a-foreign-language-in-school-while-americans-lag/

Pilon, S. (2017). Developing intercultural learning among students in short-term study abroad programs. *NECTFL Review, February* (79),133–153. www.nectfl.org/wp-content/uploads/2017/02/NECTFL-SPECIAL-ISSUE.pdf

Pizzolato, J. E. (2005). Creating crossroads for self-authorship: Investigating the provocative moment. *Journal of College Student Development, 46*(6), 624–641. https://psycnet.apa.org/doi/10.1353/csd.2005.0064

Ramirez, E. (2016). Impact on intercultural competence when studying abroad and the moderating role of personality. *Journal of Teaching in International Business, 27*(2–3), 88–105. https://doi.org/10.1080/08975930.2016.1208784

Redmond, M. V. & Bunyi, J. M. (1991). The relationship of intercultural communication competence with stress and the handling of stress as reported by international students. *International Journal of Intercultural Relations, 17*, 235–254. http://dx.doi.org/10.1016/0147-1767(93)90027-6

Reichard, R. J. et al. (2015). Engagement in cultural trigger events in the development of cultural competence. *Academy of Management Learning & Education, 14*(4), 461–481. https://doi.org/10.5465/amle.2013.0043

Rexeisen, R. J. & Al-Khatib, J. (2009). Assurance of learning and study abroad: A case study. *Journal of Teaching in International Business, 20*(3), 192–207. https://doi.org/10.1080/08975930903099077

Rexeisen, R. J., Anderson, P. H., Lawton, L., & Hubbard, A. C. (2008). Study abroad and intercultural development: A longitudinal study. *Frontiers: The Interdisciplinary Journal of Study Abroad, 17*, 1–20. https://doi.org/10.36366/frontiers.v17i1.241

Rings, G. & Allehyani, F. (2020). Personality traits as indicators of the development of intercultural communication competence. *International Journal of Curriculum and Instruction, 12*(1), 17–32.

Rivers, W. P. (1998). Is being there enough? The effects of homestay placements on language gain during study abroad. *Foreign Language Annals, 31*(4), 492–500. https://doi.org/10.1111/j.1944-9720.1998.tb00594.x

Roberts, T. G., Raulerson, B., Telg, R., Harder, A., & Stedman, N. (2019). Exploring how critical reflection can be used in a short-term study abroad experience to elicit cultural awareness and technical knowledge of agriculture students. *NACTA Journal, 63*(1), 25–31. www.nactateachers.org/attachments/article/2822/9.%20%20Roberts.pdf

Root, E. & Ngampornchai, A. (2013). I came back as a new human being. *Journal of Studies in International Education, 17*(5), 513–532. https://doi .org/10.1177/1028315312468008

Roy, A., Newman, A., Ellenberger, T., & Pyman, A. (2019). Outcomes of international student mobility programs: A systematic review and agenda for future research. *Studies in Higher Education, 44*(9), 1630–1644. https:// doi.org/10.1080/03075079.2018.1458222

Rubin, J. (2015). *Faculty guide for collaborative online international learning course development*. New York, NY: The Center for Collaborative Online International Learning. www.ufic.ufl.edu/UAP/Forms/COIL_guide.pdf

Şahin, F., Gurbuz, S., & Köksal, O. (2014). Cultural intelligence (CQ) in action: The effects of personality and international assignment on the development of CQ. *International Journal of Intercultural Relations, 39*, 152–163. https:// doi.org/10.1016/j.ijintrel.2013.11.002

Salisbury, M. H., An, B. P., & Pascarella, E. T. (2013). The effect of study abroad on intercultural competence among undergraduate college students. *Journal of Student Affairs Research and Practice, 50*(1), 1–20. https://doi .org/10.1515/jsarp-2013-0001

Salisbury, M. H., Paulsen, M. B., & Pascarella, E. T. (2010). To see the world or stay at home: Applying an integrated student choice model to explore the gender gap in the intent to study abroad. *Research in Higher Education, 51*(7), 615–640. https://doi.org/10.1007/s11162-010-9171-6

Sanford, N. (1966). *Self and society: social change and development*. New York,NY: Atherton Press.

Scally, J. (2015). Intercultural competence development in three different study abroad program types. *Intercultural Communication Studies, 24*(2), 35–60.

Schnabel, D., Kelava, A., Seifert, L., & Kuhlbrodt, B. (2015). Konstruktion und Validierung eines multimethodalen berufsbezogenen Tests zur Messung interkultureller Kompetenz [Development and validation of a job-related multimethod Test to Measure Intercultural Competence]. *Diagnostica, 61*, 3–21. http://dx.doi.org/10.1026/0012-1924/a000110

Sercu, L. (2002). Autonomous learning and the acquisition of intercultural communicative competence: Some implications for course development. *Language, Culture & Curriculum, 15*, 61–74.

Shimmi, Y. & Ota, H. (2018). "Super-short-term" study abroad in Japan: A dramatic increase. *International Higher Education, 94*, 13–15. https://doi .org/10.6017/ihe.2018.0.10559

Shiveley, J. & Misco, T. (2015). Long-term impacts of short-term study abroad: Teacher perceptions of preservice study abroad experiences. *Frontiers: The*

Interdisciplinary Journal of Study Abroad, *26*, 107–120. https://doi.org/10.36366/frontiers.v26i1.361

Sit, A., Mak, A. S., & Neill, J. T. (2017). Does cross-cultural training in post-secondary education enhance cross-cultural adjustment? A systematic review. *International Journal of Intercultural Relations*, *57*, 1–18. https://doi.org/10.1016/j.ijintrel.2017.01.001

Skrefsrud, T.-A. (2021).Why student mobility does not automatically lead to better understanding: Reflections on the concept of intercultural learning. In D. Cairns (Ed.), *The Palgrave Handbook of Youth Mobility and Educational Migration* (pp. 63–73). Basingstoke, UK: Springer. https://doi.org/10.1007/978-3-030-64235-8_7

Smith, B. & Yang, W. (2017). Learning outcomes in an interdisciplinary study abroad program: Developing a global perspective. *Journal of Family & Consumer Sciences*, *109*(1), 43–50. https://doi.org/10.14307/JFCS109.1.43

Spenader, A. & Retka, P. (2015). The role of pedagogical variables in Intercultural development: a study of faculty-led programs. *Frontiers: The Interdisciplinary Journal of Study Abroad*, *25*(1), 20–36. https://doi.org/10.36366/frontiers.v25i1.342

Spitzberg, B. H. & Changnon, G. (2009). Conceptualizing intercultural competence. In D. K. Deardorff (Ed.), *The SAGE handbook of intercultural competence* (pp. 2–52). Thousand Oaks, CA: Sage.

Stebleton, M. J., Soria, K. M., & Cherney, B. T. (2013). The high impact of education abroad: College students' engagement in international experiences and the development of intercultural competencies. *Frontiers: The Interdisciplinary Journal of Study Abroad*, *22*(1), 1–24. https://doi.org/10.36366/frontiers.v22i1.316

Steckley, M. & Steckley, J. (2021). E-volunteering as *international* experiential learning: student and community perspectives. *Canadian Journal of Development Studies / Revue canadienne d'études du eveloppement*. https://doi.org/10.1080/02255189.2021.1952856

Stemler, S., Imada, T., & Sorkin, C. (2014). Development and validation of the Wesleyan intercultural competence scale (WICS): A tool for measuring the impact of study abroad experiences. *Frontiers: The Interdisciplinary Journal of Study Abroad*, *24*(1), 25–58. https://doi.org/10.36366/frontiers.v24i1.335

Strange, H. & Gibson, H. (2020). An investigation of experiential and transformative learning in study abroad programs. *Frontiers: The Interdisciplinary Journal of Study Abroad*, *29*(1), 85–100. https://doi.org/10.36366/frontiers.v29i1.387

Sutton, R. C., Miller, A. N., & Rubin, D. L. (2014). Research design in assessing learning outcomes of education abroad programs. In M. C. Bolen (Ed.), *A guide to outcomes assessment in education abroad* (pp. 23–59). Warren, RI: The Forum on Education Abroad. https://forumea.org/wp-content/uploads/2014/08/Outcomes-Assessment.pdf

Tarchi, C., Surian, A., & Daiute, C. (2019). Assessing study abroad students' intercultural sensitivity with narratives. *European Journal of Psychology of Education, 34*(4), 873–894. https://doi.org/10.1007/s10212-019-00417-9

Templer, K. J., Tay, C., & Chandrasekar, N. A. (2006). Motivational cultural intelligence: Realistic job preview, realistic living conditions preview, and cross-cultural adjustment. *Group and Organization Management, 31*, 154–173. https://doi.org/10.1177%2F1059601105275293

Terzuolo, E. R. (2018). Intercultural development in study abroad: influence of student and program characteristics. *International Journal of Intercultural Relations, 65*, 86–95. https://doi.org/10.1016/j.ijintrel.2018.05.001

The Forum on Education Abroad (2017). *State of the field 2017*. Author. Warren, RI: The Forum on Education Abroad. https://forumea.org/wp-content/uploads/2018/03/ForumEA-State-of-the-Field-18-web-version.pdf

Tompkins, A., Cook, T., Miller, E., & LePeau, L. A. (2017). Gender influences on students' study abroad participation and intercultural competence. *Journal of Student Affairs Research and Practice, 54*(2), 204–216. https://doi.org/10.1080/19496591.2017.1284671

Thomas, K. L. & Kerstetter, D. (2020). The awe in awesome in education abroad. *Frontiers: The Interdisciplinary Journal of Study Abroad, 32*(2), 94–119. https://doi.org/10.36366/frontiers.v32i2.469

Torii, J., Fruja Amthor, R., & Murray, J. L. (2020). Two-way cultural transmission in study-abroad: U.S. host families and Japanese college students in short-term homestay programs. *Journal of Student Affairs Research and Practice, 57*(5), 578–590. https://doi.org/10.1080/19496591.2020.1726360

Tracy-Ventura, N., Dewaele, J.-M., Köylü, Z, & McManus, K. (2016). Personality changes after the "year abroad"? A mixed-methods study. *Study Abroad Research in Second Language Acquisition and International Education, 1*(1), 107–127. https://doi.org/10.1075/sar.1.1.05tra

Tsang, A. (2022). Examining the relationship between language and cross-cultural encounters: Avenues for promoting intercultural interaction. *Journal of Multilingual and Multicultural Development, 43*(2), 98–110. https://doi.org/10.1080/01434632.2020.1725526

Triandis, H. C. (1998). Introduction to diversity in clinical psychology. In A. S. Bellack & M. Hersen (Eds.), *Comprehensive clinical psychology* (pp. 1–33). New York, NY: Pergamon. https://doi.org/10.1016/B0080-4270(73)00103-6

Uhlmann, E. L. (2012). American psychological isolationism. *Review of General Psychology*, *16*(4), 381–390. https://doi.org/10.1037/a0027702

Van der Poel, M. H. (2016). When does study abroad foster intercultural competence? A study in search of the conditions. *European Journal of Cross-Cultural Competence and Management*, *4*(2), 168–185. www .inderscience.com/offer.php?id=83841

van der Zee, K. I. & Brinkmann, U. (2004). Construct validity evidence for the intercultural readiness check against the multicultural personality questionnaire. *International Journal of Selection and Assessment*, *12*(3), 285–290. https://doi.org/10.1111/j.0965-075X.2004.283_1.x

van der Zee, K. I. & Van Oudenhoven, J. P. (2000). The multicultural personality questionnaire: A multidimensional instrument of multicultural effectiveness. *European Journal of Personality*, *14*(4), 291–309. https://do.org/10.1002/1099-0984(200007/08)14:4<291::AID-PER377>3.0 .CO;2-6

van der Zee, K. & van Oudenhoven, J. P. (2013). Culture shock or challenge? The role of personality as a determinant of intercultural competence. *Journal of Cross-Cultural Psychology*, *44*(6), 928–940. https://doi.org/10.1177/ 0022022113493138

Van Mol, C. (2022). Exploring explanations for the gender gap in study abroad: a case study of the Netherlands. *Higher Education*, *83*, 441–459. https://doi .org/10.1007/s10734-020-00671-7

van Oudenhoven, J. P., Timmerman, M. E., & van der Zee, K. I. (2007). Cross-cultural equivalence and validity of the multicultural personality questionnaire in an intercultural context. *Journal of Intercultural Communication*, *13*, 51–65. https://doi.org/10.1080/13216597.2007 .9674714

van Oudenhoven, J. P. & Van der Zee, K. I. (2002). Predicting multicultural effectiveness of international students: The Multicultural Personality Questionnaire. *International Journal of Intercultural Relations*, *26*(6), 679–694. https://doi.org/10.1016/S0147-1767(02)00041-X

van Seggelen-Damen, I. & van Dam, K. (2016). Self-reflection as a mediator between self-efficacy and well-being. *Journal of Managerial Psychology*, *31*(1), 18–33. http://dx.doi.org/10.1108/JMP-01-2013-0022

Vande Berg, M., Connor-Linton, J., & Paige, R. M. (2009). The georgetown consortium project: Interventions for student learning abroad. *Frontiers: The Interdisciplinary Journal of Study Abroad*, *18*(1), 1–75. https://doi.org/ 10.36366/frontiers.v18i1.251

Vande Berg, M., Paige, R. M., & Lou, K. H. (Eds.). (2012). *Student learning abroad: What our students are learning, what they're not, and what we can do about it*. Sterling, VA: Stylus.

Varela, O. E. (2017). Learning outcomes of study-abroad programs: A meta-analysis. *Academy of Management Learning & Education, 16*(4), 531–561. https://doi.org/10.5465/amle.2015.0250

Volpone, S. D., Marquardt, D. J., Casper, W. J., & Avery, D. R. (2018). Minimizing cross-cultural maladaptation: How minority status facilitates change in international acculturation. *Journal of Applied Psychology, 103*(3), 249–269. https://psycnet.apa.org/doi/10.1037/apl0000273

Wächter, B. (2014). Recent trends in student mobility in Europe. In B. T. Streitwieser (Ed.), *Internationalisation of higher education and global mobility* (pp. 87–97). Oxford: Symposium Books.

Wang, W.-L. & Ching, G. S. (2015). The role of personality and intercultural effectiveness towards study abroad academic and social activities. *International Journal of Research Studies in Psychology, 4*(4), 13–27. http://consortiacademia.org/wp-content/uploads/IJRSP/IJRSP_v4i4/774-4531-1-PB.pdf

Ward, C. & Kennedy, A. (1993). Psychological and sociocultural adjustment during cross-cultural transitions: A comparison of secondary students at home and abroad. *International Journal of Psychology, 28*(2), 129–147. https://doi.org/10.1080/00207599308247181

Ward, C. & Kennedy, A. (1999). The measurement of sociocultural adaptation. *International Journal of Intercultural Relations, 23*(4), 659–677. https://doi.org/10.1016/S0147-1767(99)00014-0

Ward, C. & Rana-Deuba, A. (1999). Acculturation and adaptation revisited. *Journal of Cross-Cultural Psychology, 30*(4), 422–442. https://doi.org/10.1177/0022022199030004003

Ward, C., Bochner, S., & Furnham, A. (2001). *The psychology of culture shock*. New York: Routledge.

Whatley, M., Landon, A. C., Tarrant, M. A., & Rubin, D. (2021). Program design and the development of students' global perspectives in faculty-led short-term study abroad. *Journal of Studies in International Education, 25* (3), 301–318. https://doi.org/10.1177/1028315320906156

Wickline, V. B., Shae, A. M., Young, C., & Wiese, D. (2020). Increasing intercultural competence in undergraduate education: Study abroad is a viable way, but not the only way. *Frontiers: The Interdisciplinary Journal of Study Abroad, 32*(3), 126–155. https://doi.org/10.36366/frontiers.v32i3.582

Williams, T. R. (2009). The reflective model of intercultural competency: A multidimensional, qualitative approach to study abroad assessment.

Frontiers: The Interdisciplinary Journal of Study Abroad, 18(1), 289–306. https://doi.org/10.36366/frontiers.v18i1.267

Williams, T. R. (2018). *Learning through a PRISM: Facilitating student intercultural learning abroad.* Fort Worth, TX: TCU Press.

Williamson, W. (2008). *Study abroad 101.* Charleston, IL: Agapy.

Wilson, J., Ward, C., & Fischer, R. (2013). Beyond culture learning theory. *Journal of Cross-Cultural Psychology, 44*(6), 900–927. https://doi.org/10.1177/0022022113492889

Wolff, F. & Borzikowsky, C. (2018). Intercultural competence by international experiences? An investigation of the impact of educational stays abroad on intercultural competence and its facets. *Journal of Cross-Cultural Psychology, 49*(3), 488–514. https://doi.org/10.1177/0022022118754721

Wu, W. P., Fan, W. W., & Peng, R. Z. (2013). An analysis of the assessment tools for Chinese college students' intercultural competence. *Foreign Language Teaching and Research, 4,* 581–592

Yashima, T., Zenuk-Nishide, L., & Shimizu, K. (2004). The influence of attitudes and affect on willingness to communicate and second language communication. *Language Learning, 54*(1), 119–152. http://dx.doi.org/10.1111/j.1467-9922.2004.00250.x

Yu, B., Bodycott, P., & Mak, A. S. (2019). Language and interpersonal resource predictors of psychological and sociocultural adaptation: International students in Hong Kong. *Journal of Studies in International Education, 23*(5), 572–588. http://dx.doi.org/10.1177/1028315318825336

Yu, B. & Shen, H. (2012). Predicting roles of linguistic confidence, integrative motivation and second language proficiency on cross-cultural adaptation. *International Journal of Intercultural Relations, 36*(1), 72–82. https://psycnet.apa.org/doi/10.1016/j.ijintrel.2010.12.002

Zhang, X. & Zhou, M. (2019). Interventions to promote learners' intercultural competence: A meta-analysis. *International Journal of Intercultural Relations, 71,* 31–47. https://doi.org/10.1016/j.ijintrel.2019.04.006

Zimmermann, J., Greischel, H., & Jonkmann, K. (2020). The development of multicultural effectiveness in international student mobility. *Higher Education.* Advance online publication. https://doi.org/10.1007/s10734-020-00509-2

Zimmermann, J. & Neyer, F. J. (2013). Do we become a different person when hitting the road? Personality development of sojourners. *Journal of Personality and Social Psychology, 105*(3), 515–530. https://doi.org/10.1037/a0033019

Cambridge Elements ≡

Psychology and Culture

Kenneth D. Keith

University of San Diego

Kenneth D. Keith is author or editor of more than 160 publications on cross-cultural psychology, quality of life, intellectual disability, and the teaching of psychology. He was the 2017 president of the Society for the Teaching of Psychology.

About the Series

Elements in Psychology and Culture features authoritative surveys and updates on key topics in cultural, cross-cultural, and indigenous psychology. Authors are internationally recognized scholars whose work is at the forefront of their subdisciplines within the realm of psychology and culture.

Cambridge Elements ≡

Psychology and Culture

Elements in the Series

A full series listing is available at: www.cambridge.org/EPAC